Confronting al Qaeda

The Sunni Awakening and American Strategy in al Anbar

Martha L. Cottam and Joe W. Huseby

With
Bruno Baltodano

A PEPÓN Y LOURDES,

CON MUCHO CARIÑO Y CON TODO MI RESPETO,

SU NIETO, E HIJO.

BRUNO BALTODANO

ROWMAN & LITTLEFIELD
Lanham • Boulder • New York • London

Published by Rowman & Littlefield
A wholly owned subsidiary of The Rowman & Littlefield Publishing Group, Inc.
4501 Forbes Boulevard, Suite 200, Lanham, Maryland 20706
www.rowman.com

Unit A, Whitacre Mews, 26-34 Stannary Street, London SE11 4AB

Copyright © 2016 by Rowman & Littlefield

All rights reserved. No part of this book may be reproduced in any form or by any electronic or mechanical means, including information storage and retrieval systems, without written permission from the publisher, except by a reviewer who may quote passages in a review.

British Library Cataloguing in Publication Data

Library of Congress Cataloging-in-Publication Data
Names: Cottam, Martha L., author. | Huseby, Joe W., author. | Baltodano, Bruno, author.
Title: Confronting al Qaeda : the Sunni awakening and American strategy in al Anbar / by Martha L. Cottam and Joe W. Huseby with Bruno Baltodano.
Description: Lanham, Md. : Rowman & Littlefield, [2016] | Includes bibliographical references and index.
Identifiers: LCCN 2015041628| ISBN 9781442264854 (cloth : alk. paper) | ISBN 9781442264861 (electronic)
Subjects: LCSH: Iraq War, 2003-2011—Campaigns—Iraq—Anbar (Province) | Counterinsurgency—Iraq—Anbar (Province) | Qaida (Organization) | Anbar (Iraq : Province)—Politics and government—2003- | Iraq—Military relations—United States. | United States—Military relations—Iraq.
Classification: LCC DS79.764.A63 C68 2016 | DDC 956.7044/342—dc23 LC record available at http://lccn.loc.gov/2015041628

∞™ The paper used in this publication meets the minimum requirements of American National Standard for Information Sciences—Permanence of Paper for Printed Library Materials, ANSI/NISO Z39.48-1992.

Printed in the United States of America

Contents

Figures and Tables vii
Acknowledgments ix

1 Introduction 1
Explaining the Awakening 3
Social Identity Themes 4
Identities in al Anbar 5
The Role of Images 11
Methodology 16

2 US Intervention and the Birth of the Insurgency in al Anbar 23
Introduction 23
American Image of Iraq; President George W. Bush and His Administration 23
L. Paul Bremer, the Coalition Provisional Authority, and de-Ba'athification 30
The US Military: Mistakes, Regrets, and Early Corrections 35
Abu Ghraib 39
Fallujah 42
Ramadi 45

3 The Tribes: High Expectations and Disappointment 47
Preparing al Anbar for the Americans 49
One Last Try 56
The Insurgency 59
Explanations and Summary 62
Threats to Sunni Tribal Identity by the United States 62
Tribal Image of the United States 64
Sunni Tribal Image of al Qaeda 2003–2004 64

American Images of the Sunni Tribes 65
Conclusion 66

4 The Violence Escalates 69
Conspiracy Thinking and Perceptions of Iran and the Shi'a 74
Early Signs of Revolt: Al Qaim 76
The Americans Change Strategy 83
Implementing the New Strategy 86
Moving Toward an Awakening 92
Tenets of the Awakening Meeting 93
Conclusion 94

5 The Awakening Spreads 97
Conclusion 111

6 Epilogue and Conclusions 115
Security in Iraq and Al-Anbar 116
Military Progress Followed by Political Failings 117
Fracturing of the Iraqiya Party 118
Resurgent Sunni Militants and Fundamentalists 119
Replicating the Awakening 125
Conclusions 130

References 137

Index 143

About the Authors 147

Figures and Tables

Figure 1.1	Political Images and Strategic Preferences	13
Figure 4.1	Sunni Images before, during and after the Awakening	95
Table 1.1	Operative Tribal Images in Anbar	13
Table 5.1	Civilian Deaths Caused by Insurgents	111
Table 5.2	Civilian Deaths by All Combatants	111

Acknowledgments

The authors would like to acknowledge and thank first our interviewees for providing us with extraordinary information and insight into the Awakening. We also thank the funding agency that made the interviews possible, and Max and Abdullah, our translator and driver, respectively. Friends and colleagues who provided us with ideas and critical reviews include Nicole Burtchett Drumhiller, Alyssa Deffenbaugh, Elena Mastors, Tom Preston and the Kruzel brownbag group, Craig Whiteside, and our students.

Chapter 1

Introduction

By 2004, al Anbar Province in Iraq was one of the most dangerous places for American forces in Iraq. The province, which comporises one-third of Iraqi territory, was wracked with violence committed by Iraqi national insurgent groups, and increasingly by the al Qaeda branch, al Qaeda in Iraq (AQI). The province seemed all but lost to insurgency and AQI violence and with little prospect for political integration with Baghdad and the rest of the country. Yet, by the spring of 2005 a dramatic change began, as the Bedouin tribes of al Anbar began gradually to resist AQI, and join forces with American Army and Marine forces. The vital turning of the tide began in the district of al Qaim when the Albu Mahal tribe launched an attack against AQI. This was the initial volley in what would eventually become known as the Sunni Awakening, or *Sahawa*, in Arabic. It reflected not only a profound shift in the Sunni tribes' strategy in violence-torn al Anbar Province, but it also resulted ultimately in close cooperation with American forces in an effort to rid al Anbar of AQI. The tribes faced threats on three fronts: they were being targeted by AQI; they were increasingly marginalized by politicians in Baghdad; and they were being disarmed by US-led forces. The tribes viewed those forces as disrespectful intruders who had no desire to work with the tribes. Their eventual decision to engage, in a united front, militarily with AQI and then to eventually partner with US forces was a very risky strategy. It did not come without cost, however. They knew this strategy was certain to result in the deaths of many tribal leaders and members as they fought AQI.

This risky change in strategy on the part of the tribes could not have been more welcomed by the American forces, who were facing a rising insurgency and deepening sectarian conflict in Iraq. Like the Sunni tribes in al Anbar, they too underwent a change in strategy between 2004 and 2005, recognizing that their initial tough approach to the Sunnis backfired and produced insurgency instead of acceptance of the new order. The American military forces gradually developed a new counterinsurgency strategy for al Anbar, and began to encourage cooperation with the tribal leaders. The Americans and the tribes developed a mutually beneficial relationship in which the US forces would provide training for police and army members, as well as contracts to the tribes to build schools, restore electricity, irrigation, and many other facilities. In exchange, the tribes provided recruits for the army and police, and crucial intelligence, while they fought AQI in the al Anbar region.

This newfound alliance between the tribes and American forces proved highly effective in combating AQI and in reducing the insurgent violence. By teaming local knowledge of the tribal defense forces with American military resources, AQI was rather quickly deposed in the province. How did this alliance come about? How did two groups, who regarded one another with suspicion and hostility, change their perceptions, engage in risky cooperation, and defeat a ferocious opponent? By 2008 AQI was severely damaged in al Anbar, and the province was relatively peaceful. Eventually, exiles began to return, and the Sunnis participated more fully in the political process in Baghdad.

This book is a study of decision-making process and the political psychology of the Sunni Awakening in al Anbar and the change in American military strategy that made the Awakening a collaboration between the Sunni tribes and the US forces. We describe the change in the tribal leaders' perspective and the change in American military strategy as two vectors with different origins that came together successfully to defeat AQI in al Anbar. Much of the study relies upon interviews with Iraqis and Americans involved in the Awakening, and the story is often told through their words. Our explanation for this phenomenon is based on political psychology, specifically, the effects of changing perceptions, or images, of one another, and the dynamics of social identity. Political and military realities threatened Sunni identity and forced the perceptual shifts initially, and later the process of cooperation and engagement accelerated these shifts through increasingly mutually beneficial interaction during pitched battles with AQI. On the American side, officers on the ground realized that their early approach to the Iraqis was not effective and, through trial and error, found a new more effective strategy.

The book is organized as follows: In this chapter, we will introduce the readers to al Anbar Province. Tribal make-up, the historical interaction of the tribes with the central Iraqi government, the efforts made by Saddam Hussein to influence the tribes, and their interests at the time of the US incursion will be discussed. Attention to tribal dynamics—competition and collaboration, variations in size and prestige, and values and norms—will also be covered. We will conclude the chapter with the analytical factors that will be used to explain the Awakening phenomenon, as well as a review of the methodology used in the research.

Chapter 2 examines the political and military strategy employed by the United States at the beginning of Operation Iraqi Freedom, from conventional military maneuvers to de-Ba'athification policies. Chapter 3 examines the Sunni tribal expectations about their role in the future Iraq as well as their perceptions of the Americans. It also discusses early tribal efforts to negotiate with the Americans and the emergence of the insurgency,

Chapter 4 examines the important shift in mutual images that enabled the Americans and the tribal leaders to trust each other and collaborate rather than rebuff proposals of cooperation as they had in the earlier stages of the process. Chapter 4 also explores leadership issues in the tribes, and the American gamble in producing incentives, promoting competition among the tribes while at the same time maintaining their cooperation with each other and the Americans in the midst of the violence in al Anbar. The focus of chapter 5 is the learning curve involved in the American approach to the tribes and the spread of the Awakening across the province.

Chapter 6 concludes with a discussion of lessons learned from this case, an analysis of al Anbar after the Awakening, and briefly addressing whether the strategies that worked in al Anbar will work elsewhere. We will argue that while many of these lessons are not directly applicable to other areas experiencing insurgency or instability triggered by non-state actors, general patterns identified in the case can be instructive for other complicated tribal situations. The concluding chapter also examines the present situation in al Anbar. Current tribal and AQI (ISIS) relations are reviewed with the lessons learned from recent history of this study as the backdrop.

EXPLAINING THE AWAKENING

The Awakening has not received much scholarly attention. Consequently, there are few competing explanations of it to review. One explanation, chiefly promoted by Long (2009), is that the tribes had a financial incentive to participate in the Awakening. Financial motivation and material resources are certainly a motivating factor and a partial explanation of participation in the Awakening movement. As will be seen when the book unfolds the details of the Awakening, the tribes did benefit financially from their participation in the Awakening. However, when one considers the tremendous risks that participation involved, the high death rates and losses of entire families in some cases, the financial incentive could hardly have been sufficient to have been the primary factor motivating the Awakening. Beyond the acquisition of resources and financial gain, increased security derived from cooperating with the Americans did play a role in motivating participation in the Awakening, but the history of the movement shows that the tribes were going to fight AQI with or without US support. Moreover, understanding the Awakening through the motivations and psychology of the tribes is only part of the story. A fuller examination requires not only an explanation of the tribes' behavior and their strategic choices, but also an examination of the change in American strategy and perceptions. The tribes are only half of the equation. We maintain that the tribes changed because of the fundamental threat posed by AQI to their survival as a social group and because of changes in their images of both the United States and AQI. In tandem, American forces, particularly the leadership, changed their perception, or image, of the Sunni tribes. This change was also spurred by threats, previously unsuccessful tactics, and increased contextual knowledge applied to strategy. This change in perception prompted a change in strategy on the ground in al Anbar. Both sides of the equation experienced a shift in images of the other groups that explains critical changes in policy and strategy that led to eventual success. Given this assertion, it is time to develop our analytical factors in more detail.

SOCIAL IDENTITY THEMES

Social identity theory is one theory from political psychology that will be used to explain the evolutions of the Awakening. Social identity studies assert four central propositions (Tajfel, 1970; 1978; 1982; Tajfel & Billig, 1974). First, people strive to maintain positive self-images. This means that people want to see themselves in a positive light when they are comparing themselves to others. Second, membership in groups contributes to the individual's identity and self-image. Belonging to groups is important to people because they are social animals. People need groups for survival, for security, and for companionship. Third, individuals evaluate their own groups by comparing them with other groups. Finally, positive individual social identity is contingent upon a positive comparison of one's own with other groups. The link between the self and in-groups is quite complex. While people derive positive self-evaluations from group membership, they also use positive information about the self to form positive expectancies for the groups they belong to. People compare their own group with other groups, but the important comparison is with other *relevant* groups. People want to be equal or superior to those relevant groups, but people will accept inferiority and disadvantage when the comparison group is not seen as similar, that is when the comparison is not relevant. When the comparison is not positive, three strategies are possible: (1) Individuals can leave their group and join a better one. This is not possible in tribal society. (2) They can change the basis of the comparison. This also is not possible in conditions of violence where al Qaeda was determined to destroy the tribal structure. (3) They can attempt to compete with other groups, and change the social and/or political structure. This, it will be seen, was the only choice the tribes had.

As discussed earlier, many sacrifices and great losses were incurred for participation in the Awakening and its struggle against AQI. These risks and consequences were well known to the groups and leaders upon considering the formation of the Awakening movement. Many of the interview subjects recount in substantial detail the personal and close familial and tribal losses incurred at the time of the formation of the Awakening movement and organized resistance commenced. These choices can be explained with Social Identity theory. A critical aspect of Social Identity theory is the tendency to sacrifice for the sake of the group. Social identity studies find that people may place the group interests above their own and are very sensitive to threats to the group's well-being. Threats to the very existence of the group can produce actions that require great sacrifice, including the risk of life (Tajfel, 1970; 1978; 1982; Moghaddam, 2006; Cottam et al., 2010). Those threats can be real, as in physical violence targeted at the elimination of an entire group, or perceived threats caused by humiliation, loss of status, or marginalization of the group. The research presented here illustrates how and why tribal leaders experienced all of those threats. The interview subjects recount being faced with violent elimination through assassination, intimidation, and humiliation through acts of terrorism by AQI. The subjects also recount being confronted with humiliation, marginalization, and loss of status in their regional area and in the Baghdad political process because of policies and tactics implemented by the US occupational force. Social identity research also suggests that normally competitive groups faced with a common enemy can unite and form an alliance against that enemy. Groups that adopt a common superordinate identity can also unite to work for common goals (Cottam et al., 2010; Gaertner et al., 1993).

IDENTITIES IN AL ANBAR

To understand social identity dynamics in al Anbar, it is important to take a brief look at the values, norms, and structures of the Bedouin tribes that dominated al Anbar. One of the central aspects of life in modern-day Iraq is the predominant role played by Arab tribes[1] whose origin predates the birth of the state in 1921 (Dawisha, 2009) and which provide the foundation for political organization at the local, regional, and state level in Iraq (Charrad, 2011, and Stolzoff, 2009). Iraq has approximately 150 identifiable tribes comprising about 2,000 clans (CIA Factbook, 2013) and each tribe is distinct from the other tribes not only in name but also in terms of sociopolitical capabilities. Even as the tribes vary in size, location, and relative power, traditional tribal institutions and practices bind them and help to intensify the relationship between the individual and his or her lineage (Sakai, 2003). Al Anbar is home to the Dulaym tribal confederation, although some tribes outside of that confederation also reside in the province. Among the largest and most prominent tribes in Anbar are the Albu Nimr, Albu Issa, Albu Mahal, and the Albu Fahd.

In this brief section on tribal dynamics, we explore four of the most important aspects of tribal life in Iraq:[2] Solidarity to the tribe (*Asabiya*), honor or prestige (*Sharaf*), reliance on politically powerful tribal leaders (*Sheikhs*), and their long-held system of reciprocal obligations from the tribe to the individual and from the individual to the tribe. We will also look at the impact of the Saddam Hussein regime on tribal dynamics.

For the sake of clarification, in terms of tribal hierarchy, Iraqi tribes are divided into smaller groups leading to the larger organization. These divisions not only permeate tribal life but also allow for differing levels of action within the group. They are as follows (Fields, 1940):

1. The smallest kinship unit is the household (*Bayt*), which is named after its senior male member.
2. The next kinship unit is the clan (*Fukhth*) or the larger patrilineal descent group.
3. The next division is the tribe itself (*Asheera*) or a politicosocial unit with limited political autonomy and sovereignty over a given territory or region linked by form larger lineages.
4. Finally, tribes sharing a common male ancestor are sometimes linked into a tribal confederations (*Qabela*).

At the local and the regional level, Iraqi tribes should be understood to be traditional, autonomous political units bound only by the perceived status and power of their respective Sheikhs, a condition that has persisted and evolved since the period of post–World War I British colonialism and the artificial creation of a constitutional monarchy (Jabar, 2003). Modern Iraqi tribes share a multitude of connections (including economic, social, and political ties), but we argue that, at the local and regional level, they are able to demand and maintain primary *political loyalty* with their tribal group. At the state or national level, Iraqi tribes should be understood to function within the context of a persistent search for balance of power between them and the Iraqi central government: a complex and fluctuating condition that has proven threatening (to both) at varying points in the history of the nation, particularly during the regime of Saddam Hussein and the Ba'athist party (Charrad, 2011). This competition between local and state power is seldom at equilibrium and was taxed to extreme levels during the period of occupation that preceded the Sunni Awakening. Moreover, competition for resources, power, and prestige is also a fundamental aspect of intertribal behavior in Iraq (Dawisha, 2003). Finally, all of these aspects of daily and political life in Iraq must be understood within the context of *Asabiya* or a system of set relationships based on duty, rights and obligations, loyalty, and tribal bonds (Stolzoff, 2009).

Some of the aforementioned traditional tribal institutions and practices must be placed within the proper context in order to understand the development and dynamics of the Awakening. To begin with, the concept of *Asabiya* or tribal solidarity, foreign to most Western culture, is best understood in terms of status and group roles. It is not simply "kinship ties" as it also demands loyalty based on social connections. The following are the principal characteristics of *Asabiya* (Cole, 1975, Asad, 1970 and Abu-Lughod, 1986):

1. It demands that tribal members support one another against outsiders.
2. It provides legitimacy for actions taken in the protection or security of the tribe.
3. It is a prerequisite of tribal leadership, which, in turn, ensures protection and security to the individuals.
4. It is the foundation for *primary political loyalty*.

In other words, unlike kinship ties, *Asabiya* can amalgamate obligations between individuals having little to no lineage connection and can help to establish friendly relationships between unrelated groups.[3] There are several forms of *Asabiya* beyond the broad "tribal" solidarity (Bin Sayeed, 1995): These include "blood (e.g., Shouka, 2010)," "protection (e.g., Hamdani, 2010)," and "alliance (e.g., Khirbit, 2010)." *Asabiya* is a device with which cooperation can occur between groups that have no lineage connections. It is of primordial importance during war and armed conflict wherein the political autonomy and/or survival of the tribe are threatened. Tribes and outside groups cooperate through *Asabiya* primarily in order to strengthen their military capabilities. It requires that allies defend each other against mutual enemies (Bin Sayeed, 1995; Stolzoff, 2009; Dawisha, 1999). During these times, intermarriages serve to strengthen new coalitions and relationships outside of family lineage (Joseph, 2003).[4] It is important to recognize not only that *Asabiya* is a complex system of kinship, fictive and artificially, relations but that, most importantly, to the tribes and their individual members it is a sacred ritual.

The most important role in the tribe is that of the tribal chief or "sheikh." Traditionally, tribal decision making links the individual groups ultimately to the sheikh (Cole, 1975). The relationship between the sheikh and the members of his tribe is based on mutual respect and devotion (Abu-Lughod,

1986). On the idealized basis of these ties, the sheikh is treated as a father and obedience to him is considered to be evidence of respect, as opposed to fear and/or weakness (Levy, 1962). This leadership role demands an intimate acquaintance with the social life of the tribe. The sheikh acts as a leader in war and peace and is in charge of the business dealings of the tribe; moreover, his perceived legitimacy as the judicial authority affords him a uniquely powerful role in conflict resolution (Asad, 1970). Clan leaders and family elders act as arbitrators and indirect rulers on behalf of the sheikh. Related to the relative power and clout of a given sheikh is honor or distinction (*Sharaf*) not only for the tribal chief but also for the tribe itself.[5]

Status refers to a tribe's rank in relative comparison to others in the tribal hierarchy. There is considerable variation among the tribes in terms of status, but status is not a rigid condition (Dawisha, 2009 and Sakai, 2003). There seems to be a tangible accord in Iraqi tribes as to the criterion of what makes a high- or low-tiered tribe (Sheik Majid interview, 2010): Number of tribal members, reputation, business acumen, size of its territory, and maintenance of *Asabiya* (especially *blood Asabiya*). A high-tiered tribe (and by extension its members) is respected and feared. And the opposite is also true. In tribal life, personal relations are of paramount importance. The concepts of honor and its opposite (shame) are thus a constant preoccupation, and serve to control political behavior of tribes and individuals. *Sharaf* has to be constantly asserted or vindicated. A sheikh's share of honor is determined by his own behavior and that of his tribesmen and women, and it can either be gained or lost, based on the actions of the individual, the sheikh or the tribe. (Abu-Lughod, 1986).

Reducing or increasing the authority and *Sharaf* of the sheikhs has long been a successful political strategy in Iraq (Jabar, 2003), beginning with the British colonial power, as recognition of a given sheikh by the central government clarified and strengthened his position, prestige, and clout (Sakai, 2003 and Charrad, 2011). This interdependence served the interests of both tribal autonomy and of a central government state trying to control tribal territories. Thus, throughout the history of Iraq, lower-tiered tribes have increased their status by their association with the central government or by acquiring additional power or prestige. Status is also linked to *Sharaf.* A leader of a high-tiered tribe loses status if he becomes dependent on or is obligated to a lower-tiered sheikh.[6]

In terms of the traditional system of tribal obligations, the bond between an individual and his/her lineage is reciprocal. As mentioned before, during times of conflict, the individual's identification with lineage and tribal connections is evidence of his/her loyalty to the group and, most importantly, vice versa. During times of conflict and threats to the group, the tribe acts as one political entity (Charrad, 2011), hostile relations with outsiders and threats to tribal security demand cooperation among all levels of the tribe. This reciprocal association provides for both, the individual and the tribe, confidence and assurance of a certain degree of security (Stolzoff, 2009). In order to preserve this symbiosis, individuals must give primary political loyalty to the tribe, under all circumstances (Asad, 1970). Traditionally, the realization that tribal loyalty is well rewarded with security and personal benefits leaves the individual with marked respect and admiration for the perceived "honor" bestowed upon this relationship (Abu-Lughod, 1986) and serves to intensify the emotional bond to the household, clan, and tribe (Levy, 1962).

The relationship between the tribes and the Iraqi state has always been complicated. The state has lacked a social base since independence. As Jabbar (2000: 29) put it, the Iraqi state was a "state in search of a nation." The monarchy tried to develop an association with the traditional groups, and neglected the potential for political support from the middle and working classes, while the Ba'ath regimes did the opposite. During times of relatively high tribal political autonomy, the sheikh plays a central role in conflict resolution and planning (Dawisha, 2009). This traditional system was artificially thwarted during the regime of Sadddam Hussein (Jabar, 2003) to the extent that he outlawed tribal tribunals and tribal war councils (Dawisha, 1999), all in order to emphasize the lower status of the tribes vis-à-vis the state. The Ba'ath Party was strongly opposed to tribalism, which it regarded as a lasting vestige of feudalism and an impediment to socialism (Haddad, 2011). However, political realities were that the Ba'ath Party members, including Saddam Hussein when he came to power, were tribal members, and relied upon tribal support in promoting their own political power. By the time of the Iran-Iraq war, the Ba'ath official position on tribalism changed dramatically as tribes "came to be represented as carrying the undiluted epitome of Arab values" (Haddad, 2011: 95). Jabbar (2000) argues that following a period of instability in the 1960s, the second Ba'ath takeover in 1968 attempted to explicitly use tribal loyalties to cement itself in power. The party rapidly expanded membership in the party in the 1970s, giving Saddam Hussein, when he came to power, the ability to "literally buy elements of the various poor extended families and clans in the Sunni areas of Iraq" (p. 30), which, of course, included al Anbar province. Contracts were awarded to some families, turning them into wealthy clans and giving them more political power. This distorted normal tribal functioning, because members of tribes who were party apparatchiks began to play the role normally played by sheikhs.

The regime also took advantage of tribal and Arab identity during the Iran-Iraq war. Shi'a identity in Iraq was Iraqi, and there were important differences between the Arab Iraqi Shi'a and the Persian Shi'a of Iran. Thus, the regime was able to rely upon the "marsh Arabs" in particular who fought against the Iranians during the war.

Moreover, the state continued to woo and support tribes, which, in exchange for their loyalty to the regime, enhanced the power and identity of the tribes in a period of "re-tribalization." This was not always an easy process: tribes themselves had changed through "migration, diverging economic and social interests and changes in lifestyles and value systems [which had] almost wiped out the old cultural-spatial markers of the clan or the tribe" (Jabar, 2000: 31). Through the 1990s, Saddam encouraged the reconstruction of clans and tribal extended families in their ancestral lands. In other areas, the government allowed the manufacture of new "tribal" groups based on economic ties. Where the initiative was weak, Saddam encouraged prominent citizens to take the initiative, often producing "fake sheikhs" or permitted nonleading families to manufacture a new tribal entity in order to gain power and wealth. This created a new relationship: the state advanced the favored tribes, and who in turn, were coerced into protecting the state. Sunni-Shi'a tensions rose during this period, the regime also increased its control by relying on tribal loyalties among both Sunni and Shi'a Arabs. Saddam's rationale for increasingly relying on the tribes during this period was twofold. First, Bedouin tribal Arabs, although they had become settled, were considered the most pure Arab, thus lending strong legitimacy to his claim to power. Second, portraying the tribes as a symbol of patriotism and broadcasting popular tribal war poetry helped to forge a strong nationalistic sentiment in the populace.

Despite these distortions of normal tribal structure, status, and income, things changed dramatically after the Gulf War loss, the uprising in 1991 after the loss, and as a consequence of the sanctions imposed on Iraq after the war. The tribes became increasing important for three reasons. According to Haddad (2011),

> Firstly, by 1991 the state had had a tribal recruitment policy in many key sectors especially within the security services; furthermore, tribal networks had long-since dominated party structures. . . . Secondly, the events of 1991 showed the party at its weaest as it completely failed to resist the uprisings; the tribes were therefore seen as an agent to be worked with and through in the countryside where the state's grip was perhaps less secure. . . . Finally, the fact of the state's collapse in 1991 saw Iraqis revert to the tribe and saw the tribe step into the vacuum created by the absence of the state; that this galvanization of the tribes' status and role became a permanent feature was due to the regimes fostering of tribal identities since the 1990s for its own purposes. (p. 96)

The Iraqi state, as Haddad (2011: 97) put it, became "senile." Under the impact of international sanctions, the state disintegrated, and had less and less influence outside of Baghdad. Without the state's resources and services, people turned to their tribes, which traditionally provided security, sustenance, and identity (Jabbar, 1998; Haddad, 2011). But the state also turned to the tribes, using declarations of tribal loyalty to the regime as a form of propaganda. As Haddad notes, "tribes and tribal values were given unprecedented coverage and importance in the 1990s as a central pillar of Iraqi identity and as central pillars of the state" (2011: 99). Despite these efforts, however, during the 1990s the legitimacy of the state, which is not the equivalent of support for the regime, crumbled, as the state was decreasingly able to meet the needs of the citizens. Thus, the state gave tribes a political meaning, which became stronger as the state declined, and people looked to their tribes as the course of safety. The tribes remained competitive, often employing tribal justice at the expense of the laws of the state, and in many areas of Iraq, al Anbar in particular, they were engaged in illegal activities themselves.

From a political psychology standpoint, groups that are always competing for resources, power, and prestige are unlikely to cooperate; they will see competitors different from their own group; and they will engage in stereotyping (Cottam et al., 2010). As we have previously discussed, given the importance of competition, it is not surprising that tribes are much attuned to the resources, power, and prestige they and others can acquire. During the de-Ba'athification process, the Sunni tribes lost resources, power, and prestige. Early efforts to engage with the United States demonstrated a willingness to set aside tribal rivalries in order not only to encourage the occupation forces to work with them but also to protect their tribal status. Combined efforts by the Awakening and the American military forces allowed the tribes the freedom to create new alliances and, therefore, the tribes started to once again share a superordinate goal; namely, ridding the Province of AQI in order to protect the tribal system as a whole. The role played by the United States in enabling the tribes to create a superordinate identity and pursue the goal of fighting AQI, under the devices of The Awakening, will be the subject of the next chapter.

THE ROLE OF IMAGES

The psychological foundation of image theory begins with the argument made by psychologists that the informational environment people live in is too complex to be processed completely. Consequently, people use cognitive "short cuts" to enable them to process the most important information in that environment and to ignore the rest. The "short cuts" are a result of subconscious compartmentalization of the environment into perceptually useful cognitive categories. The categories must be "cognitively efficient," in that they allow the perceiver enough information about the perceived stimulus to make decisions, but not so much information that the perceiver is overwhelmed by it (Cottam, 1986, 1994; Cottam, 1977; Cottam & Cottam, 2001; Herrmann,

1985a; 1988; 1991). The social and political environments follow the same pattern: people form categories that enable them to process information about that environment efficiently. Images function very much as stereotypes do. The images may not reflect real characteristics of the actors, but they are strongly held and resistant to information, indicating that reality is different from the perception.

It has been argued that the political environment is categorized through images of the enemy, ally, colonial/client (sometimes referred to as a dependent), rogue, imperialist, barbarian, degenerate, and neutral. The most important informational elements of these images include information about their intentions, capability, cultural sophistication, and decision-making patterns (multiple groups involved or a small elite), all of which, in turn, make an image associated with a political context of threat or opportunity. Subsequent studies (e.g., Cottam, Baltodano & Garcia, 2011; Jackson, 2001) have found these images to be relevant to domestic political relationships (political parties, insurgent groups, tribes, etc.), as well as international state-to-state relationships. Political actors are assessed, placed in an image category, and then the image provides information about the actor, allowing the perceiver to ignore the unique aspects of that actor. In this way, images provide a heuristic for processing information in a more efficient way for the perceiver. The actor's behavioral predispositions are predicted based on the image through which the actor is perceived.

In this study, several images are seen to affect tribal perceptions of other actors—the imperialist, the barbarian, the rogue, the ally, and the enemy. Their characteristics are displayed in Table 1.1.

These are simplified perceptions, but many studies have demonstrated their existence and importance in decision making cross-culturally (e.g., Cottam, 1977; Cottam, 1986; 1994; Cottam et al., 2010; Hermann, 1985a,b; 1988; Herrmann et al., 1997; Parker, 1994).

Importantly, there are specific behavioral predispositions associated with each of these images, depicted in Figure 1.1.

In this book, five images will appear and will be used to understand the behavior of the various actors. The research will also illustrate a great deal of surprisingly rapid image changes that occurred in al Anbar province from 2003 to 2006. The images that will appear are as follows:

The Enemy Image

This image appears in the Iraqi tribal perception of Iran. The interview subjects reveal a consistent pattern of perceiving Iran in all of the hallmark characteristics of the Enemy image. It is perhaps the most pervasive and prominent image present in the interviews. The Enemy image is an image of a country

Table 1.1 Operative Tribal Images in Anbar

Image	*Characteristics*
Imperialist	An imperialist country is perceived to be superior in culture and capability, but its intentions can be either harmful or benevolent. The imperialist can operate through a "hidden hand." Either way, imperialists are a dominating people, and resisting them would be very difficult. Preferred approach toward the imperialist—submit until it weakens, then revolt.
Barbarian	Barbarians are superior in capability and inferior in culture. They are also harmful and aggressive in intentions, which make them very frightening. Preferred approach toward a barbarian—find allies to enhance capabilities.
Rogue	The rogue is inferior in capability and culture, but is also very harmful in their intentions. This is the "bad seed," the irresponsible child, who, it is believed, can and should be punished until they reform their ways. Preferred approach—crush.
Ally	The ally is perceived as equal in terms of its capability and culture, but also as very similar to your own group in values. The intentions of an ally are believed to be good. Their decision-making process is seen as complex. Preferred approach—negotiate; act together.
Enemy	Enemies are equal in cultural sophistication and capability, their intentions are harmful, they have a small decision-making elite capable of finely orchestrating decisions. Given their capability and equality, direct confrontation has only a 50/50 chance of success. Preferred approach—contain to prevent power enhancement.

Image of Other Political Actor		**Threat/Opportunity**		**Strategic Preference**
Enemy image	→	Threat high	→	Containment
Barbarian image	→	Threat high	→	Search for allies, augment power
Imperial image	→	Threat high	→	Submit/ revolt when possible
Rogue image	→	Threat moderate/low	→	Crush
Degenerate image	→	Opportunity high/ moderate	→	Challenge, take risks
Colonial Image	→	Opportunity high	→	Control, exploit
Ally Image	→	Threat/Opportunity (Will help in either context)	→	Negotiate agreements, Common strategy

Figure 1.1 Political Images and Strategic Preferences

that is equal to the perceiver's country in capability and culture, and harmful in its intentions toward the perceiver's state. The enemy is perceived to be ruled by a small, monolithic elite, but one that can cleverly strategize policies that will attempt to hurt the perceiver's country or group. In its most extreme form, the enemy image causes the perceiver to view the opponent as simply and ineluctably aggressive in motivation, monolithic in decisional structure, highly rational in decision making, and able to generate and orchestrate multiple complex conspiracies. It is often assumed that citizens who do not share this image are traitors or dupes of the enemy. The tactics used in responding to such a state can be wide ranging. Such tactics may be global or regional in focus. But the tactics tend to be competitive and noncompromising because it is believed that one cannot trust such an actor to keep its word. Clearly, this image has critical consequences for political compromise and the prospects for democratic governance if members of a shared political community view another group as agents of the enemy image. This consequence will be seen in play throughout the interviews analyzed in this text and in the more recent developments in al Anbar and its political relationships with Baghdad.

Because the enemy is as powerful and capable as the perceiver's country (or group), and is equally culturally sophisticated, there is an even chance of losing if the approach to the conflict is entirely zero-sum. Therefore, the logical option for protecting against the perceived enemy would be a strong, aggressive defense. If such a defense would eliminate the enemy, so much the better. Given the enemy's equality, direct confrontation would likely produce a 50/50 chance of failure. Therefore, a strategy of containment may be the only recognized alternative in most political contexts. In addition, when mirror enemy images exist and each side tries to contain the other through deterrence, spiral conflicts can occur in which hostility escalates rapidly and arms races occur. Good examples of the ideal-typical enemy image are the American image of the Third Reich and of the Soviet Union.

The Ally Image

This image also plays an important role in two parts of the story of al Anbar. The ally image is the initial Sunni tribal image of AQI in the period of time leading up to the 2003 invasion. A number of the interview subjects detail how they initially viewed the AQI fighters as allies in the sense that they viewed their intentions to be "good" and "helpful" in an impending political crisis. It is also the final American image of the Sunni tribes of al Anbar, as they shifted toward cooperation rather than confrontation and exclusion with the tribes. An ally image is the reverse of the enemy image. An ally is perceived to be equal in terms of its capability and culture but also very similar to the perceiver's own group in terms of values. The intentions of an ally are believed to be good and helpful. Allies are associated with threat, in that they are needed and reliable when the perceiver's country is threatened. This helps explain why Sunni tribes initially perceived the AQI fighters as allies, especially after their attempts to work with US forces were rebuffed. Allies are also associated with perceptions of opportunity when the allied relationship promises success in joint operations or in trade agreements. Contrary to the monolithic view of the Enemy's leadership and decision structure, the decision structure in the ally image is one of a complex structure with multiple groups involved in decision making. This is a product of two factors: First, people see the complexity of their own decision-making structure and, second, they assume that those they like are much like themselves. The typical approach to a country in the ally image is one of negotiation and compromise. An example of an ally image would be the American image of Great Britain or Canada. Of course, those two countries are not as powerful as the United States, but that is merely an illustration of the extent to which capability is not based upon military prowess, but is more of a perception that they will support and come to the defense of the perceiver's country.

The Barbarian Image

After the initial stage of viewing AQI as an ally, the tribes transitioned to perceiving AQI in the barbarian category.[7] This replacement of the ally image with the barbarian image occurred in late 2004. The barbarian image appears when an intense threat is perceived to be emanating from a political entity viewed as superior in terms of capability but as inferior culturally. Barbarians are also aggressive and harmful in intentions, which make them very dangerous and associated with a high threat perception to the perceivers. Because of that perceived capability asymmetry, the policy predisposition would be to search for powerful protectors (allies in the normal, non-image-based use of the term). This would offset the capability difference, but it does not lead to capability symmetry, because the perceiver's state does not have complete control of the capability base. The allies would have to be convinced that the barbarian offers some threat to their own national interests. The barbarian image appeared historically in the Chinese, Greek, and Roman descriptions of their tribal tormentors. Today, it is reflected in the Israeli image of the Arab world and is found within numerous countries in minority communities that are relatively highly achieving and that view their neighbors as threatening. An example of the latter is the Croatian image of the Serbs as Yugoslavia disintegrated.

The Imperial Image

This image was the one the tribes had of the Americans in 2003 and it lasted until 2006. An actor classified in the imperial image is perceived to have a dominating culture and to be superior in capability. Its intentions are harmful, although those sectors of society that benefit from it will perceive it as benevolent, as the Sunni tribes did of America before and shortly after the invasion. It is associated with threat. The classical form of the imperial image can be found in the colonial era, but it still exists today in the perception of neocolonialism held by many people in Third World countries. Actors perceived through the imperial image are perceived to be motivated by the desire to exploit the resources of the perceiver's country and to do so by forcing the perceiver's people into political and economic subservience. The decision structure of the imperial power is viewed as less monolithic than in the enemy image. Often an anti-imperial element is perceived to be present in the imperial power. The decision style of the imperial power is perceived to be adapted to the needs of an indirect control system and is subtle and discrete. The control system is perceived to be an elaborate web of institutions and individuals. On the surface, the system appears to operate through local leaders, but in fact the imperial power is perceived as pulling the strings, often at a very detailed level. The imperial power is viewed as having the capacity to orchestrate developments of extraordinary complexity and to do so with great subtlety. Because of this extraordinary ability, resistance to the imperial power is likely to prove fruitless unless there is a perception of a realistic cognitive alternative to the present situation. This occurs when the imperial power begins to be seen as a "paper tiger," which often coincides with a rise in nationalism in the perceiver's country. Examples of the imperial image can be seen in Fidel Castro's image of the United States, and in many other Latin American countries where the image of the United States is that of the imperialist.

The Rogue Image

This is the initial American image of the Sunni tribes of al Anbar. The rogue is inferior in capability and culture, but also very harmful in its intentions. The rogue is the "bad seed," the "irresponsible" child, which, it is believed, can and should be punished until it reforms its ways. The rogue image is a post–Cold War image and it replaced the dependent of the enemy image that existed during the Cold War. Responses to this type of actor are driven by a sense of superiority, hostility, and antagonism. The behavioral predispositions include a tendency to issue orders and ultimatums, and with little provocation, aggressive, often preemptive, attacks. The decision-making structure of the rogue is perceived to be a corrupt small monolithic elite. The rogue image can be seen in the Clinton and Bush administrations' perceptions of Iran, Iraq (under Saddam Hussein), North Korea, and Cuba.

METHODOLOGY

The bulk of this research is based on original data analyzed and collected by the research team. The data collection and analysis for this research was done primarily through face-to-face interviews with primary actors and decision makers among the al Anbar tribal leadership and various military leaders on the US side of the equation. The research team conducted guided interviews with 27 tribal sheikhs and other notables from the regions of Al Qaim, Ramadi and Fallujah in the al Anbar province. These interviews were conducted in Amman, Jordan. It is important to note that though the subjects were outside of Iraq, these Iraqi interviewees were not exiles in Jordan as they are Bedouins, and Bedouin tribes occupied large swaths of land in which they frequently have business and residences. These activities take them across the borders of modern states. Most of our interviewees traveled back and forth to Iraq where they still had homes. For the American perspective, the research team conducted interviews with American military officers who were in Iraq during the time period in question, and with Amman embassy officials.

The interviews followed a consistent pattern of a regimented interview of prepared questions, but there was always an allowance for follow-up questions after each prepared question. The interviews also included an "open" session after the lists of prepared questions were finished. The prepared interview questions and follow-up open-ended questions were designed to collect data relevant to the subject's social identity, the subject's perceptions of the various groups involved in events in al Anbar, and images of the various actors and groups in al Anbar and Baghdad. These questions were geared toward exploring the categorizations of the groups over time. Identities and perceptions held by the actors before, during, and after the Awakening movement were explored. These questions were aimed at collecting data on a subject's group identity, comparisons between various cognitive images held by each subject about each group and actor. That is, questions were directed toward gaining understandings of each subject's observations and perception of the other group behaviors, motivations, the threats they perceived, and the subject's understandings of various group abilities (power), intentions, and values (culture). The interviews sought to gain insight into the subject's explanations of group behaviors and the dynamics of their relationships between the various groups in al Anbar during the period of study. The research team was interested in explanations that subjects had of the choices made, not just of the subject's own group but those of the groups with which they were dealing. The questions were primarily aimed at the period just after the invasion and during the Awakening, but some questions and interviews delved into more general perceptions of groups and political actors in Iraq, al Anbar, and the international stage. These questions provide insight into assumptions of leadership structure, abilities, and intentions. The research questions also sought to explore how the subjects explain the transition of conflict. We asked the subjects why they believed relations and strategies changed over time.

The perspectives provided through these interviews help provide insight into the changing cognitive map of the perceivers, and help explain their own adaptations to a changing and threatening social and political environment. These accounts help us understand the important image shifts throughout the story of al Anbar and the Awakening. They provide insights into how the actors perceived the political and military landscape at various stages of the Awakening and the American strategic shift. Questions in the interviews also seek to explain the complexities of competition and cooperation between the tribes and how and why those obstacles were overcome through cooperation.

Not all of the data were collected through original research and interviews conducted by the authors. Our fieldwork was supplemented by interviews done by Marine historians available online and the interviews conducted by several journalists during the period under study. Whenever possible, we let the actors speak for themselves, in their own words, about the events that occurred in al Anbar Province from 2003 to 2008. For this we provide ample direct quotations from key decision makers, followed by analysis using social identity theory and image theory.

The transcripts of our interviews and those done by others are analyzed using qualitative content analysis. Statements reflecting the perceptions of our subject are examined for various characteristics relevant to image theory as detailed in Figure 1. In this framework, we pay special attention to a subject's references to the perceptions of capability, culture, intentions, decision-making patterns, and threat or opportunity presented by various groups. In the case of our interviews, interviewees were asked direct questions about these attributes in order to gain an initial assessment of perceptions. However, in follow-up questions and in the open-ended segment of the interview, the questions regarding these traits were often more oblique. The intention in these questions was to gain information through less self-monitored statements of perceptions by our subjects and thus a better, more accurate assessment of their images and perceptions held of the various groups.

The statements of our subjects were also examined for information about the interviewee's social identity. This means that we paid careful attention to how subjects identified themselves in their interviews and open-ended discussions and to how they placed themselves in their social world. This helped us understand the social cognitive map of the subjects and to help us identify to which identity the subject felt attached and to which the subject felt most closely identified. In so doing, our questions were meant to explore the depth of attachment to various social groups the subjects held. We explored the salience of various social identities. This was an effort to understand how the subject ordered their own identities and which identities the subject identified as important to themselves and others around them. The responses to these questions help us understand why decisions were made. For example, decisions involving substantial risk and self-sacrifice are better understood from the social identity perspective after the subject provides an insight into how they self-identify and how they rank that identity. A basic question the research team explored in our interview questions with tribal members was how or if the subjects rank-ordered their identity (i.e., tribal affiliation, Sunni, Muslim, Iraqi, Arab, or some other groupings of categories). These questions helped the researchers place the decisions the subjects described into a context, or map, of priorities, values, and threats (or opportunities) consistent with our theoretical framework.

The research team also analyzed secondary source material to gain a further understanding of the social identities and images at work in the Awakening. These secondary sources include archival research of news reports, journalistic accounts, documents, and articles written by military officers. These secondary sources often proved valuable in offering complementary and supportive or triangulating data that buttressed the data collected through the research team's own interviews. These sources also helped provide historical clarity in terms of the timing of events and helped pinpoint the recollections of the subjects during postinterview analysis.

Naturally there are limitations to this research. First, our data speak most specifically to events in al Qaim, Ramadi, and Fallujah districts. The tribal leaders and the American forces we interviewed were either from these areas, or, in the American cases, deployed in these regions during the time frame of our investigation. In this sense, our research does not fully account in great detail for events outside these regions, during or outside this time period. In this light, the entire Province of al Anbar is viewed in some way as reflective of the accounts and histories we collect in this research. The secondary data we collected regarding events in the greater province support the general picture we paint through the data we collected in these specific regions, giving us confidence in making generalizations about the province at large from our findings in these narrow but vital areas. Since most of the key events in the province occurred in the regions we study, we do not view this as a major limitation but one that needs mentioning at the outset. Second, the interviews sometimes give contradictory accounts of events and participants or sequencing of events. When possible, we tried to put differing accounts together for a whole picture. In general, we have been successful in triangulating various accounts to put together the full puzzle. However, at various points the discrepancies can only be stated, not explained. These discrepancies are noted when encountered. Third, we were not able to interview all of the individuals we wished to interview, and we did not get representatives from all of the important tribes. Fourth, we interviewed the elite, as did the Marine Corps in their 2009 publication. There are no data that we know of that assesses average public opinion on the issues under examination here. We have good reason to believe that the opinions expressed by the interviewees would be reflected among the wider population in al Anbar in general. However, in some cases, we note that this applicability is questionable. Finally, many people we would like to have been able to interview have died. These include some of the most important actors in the Awakening, thus leaving an important narrative untold in this account. We have attempted to bridge this gap by interviewing people closely associated or linked to the missing accounts as much as possible, and by relying on secondary sources. Nonetheless, as this research demonstrates, the personal narratives of specific actors are invaluable in understanding the Awakening, and the loss of certain accounts remains a tear in the history that cannot be fully mended, despite our efforts to bridge that gap as much as possible through alternate means. Finally, the analytical focus of this study is on elements of political psychology. This does not mean that these are the only factors affecting the events we describe below. Bureaucratic competition between the Defense Department and the CIA and Department of State are evident, as is conflict between civilians in the Defense Department and commanders on the ground trying to prevent and then defeat the insurgencies. These are described in the chapters that follow, but the analytical focus is elsewhere.

NOTES

1. The term "tribes" and "tribalism" has been a contested concept in social sciences, primarily by researchers who criticize the tendency to equate tribalism with "absence of modernity" or "lack of complexity" (e.g., Salzman, 2008). For the sake of clarification herein we use it to mean: "A sovereign, indigenous kinship group of varying size (some tribes count only for a few hundred individuals while others are more populous than some nation-states—CIA Factbook) able to demand primary loyalty based on a shared identity."

2. There are other aspects of tribal life to discuss (e.g., marriage practices, language, and economic modalities), but we will focus only on the three that played a primal role during the times preceding and leading to the Awakening.

3. This dynamic helps to understand the efficiency with which AQI was able to enter into tribal life in Iraq during the occupation by the US and the coalition forces.

4. It is not coincidental that AQI forced arranged marriages between Iraqi tribal women and members of their cadre and leadership during the early years of the occupation of Iraq by American and coalition forces.

5. It is axiomatic but important to note that Sharaf and Asabiya have a positive correlation, the more status a sheikh or a tribe can accrue the stronger the loyalty of the individual member for his/her tribe.

6. Throughout the Saddam Hussein regime, the described relationship between the sheikhs and state was a key element in the process of regime construction and

maintenance. This was done by breaking up the most powerful tribal confederations and undermining the status of their sheikhs. We discuss this in other sections of the book.

7. Some members of tribes continued to fight with AQI, so this transition to the barbarian image was not uniform. It reflects the comments made by our interviewees, who were among the tribal elite. The interviewees dismissed those who sided with AQI as "criminals" or wayward youths from bad families.

Chapter 2

US Intervention and the Birth of the Insurgency in al Anbar

INTRODUCTION

No one, neither the US policy planners nor the US military, was ready for the insurgency that began to boil in al Anbar in 2003.[1] In this chapter the origins of that insurgency will be examined, beginning with the American actions that helped provoke it, and continuing with the expectations and reactions of the tribal leaders of al Anbar. The scene is set with an exploration of the images held by President George W. Bush and his associates of the Sunnis of Iraq. Then the discussion turns to actions on the ground in Iraq as the invasion proceeded and the effort was made to pacify the country. Then we turn to the perceptions held of the United States by tribal leaders, their actions, and the nature of their support for the insurgency. These images help in understanding the behavior and decision-making process of leaders and also help understand how behaviors and specific policies were interpreted by various actors who played a key role in the insurgency and counterinsurgency.

AMERICAN IMAGE OF IRAQ; PRESIDENT GEORGE W. BUSH AND HIS ADMINISTRATION

George Bush entered office with the rogue image as an important component of his worldview. It is clearly evident in his statements after the terrorist attack on 9/11. The culprits and their allies are described in highly simplified and threatening terms:

> Americans are asking, why do they hate us? They hate what we see right here in this chamber—a democratically elected government. Their leaders are

> self-appointed. They hate our freedoms—our freedom of religion, our freedom of speech, our freedom to vote and assemble and disagree with each other. They want to overthrow existing governments in many Muslim countries, such as Egypt, Saudi Arabia, and Jordan. They want to drive Israel out of the Middle East. They want to drive Christians and Jews out of vast regions of Asia and Africa. The civilized world is rallying to America's side. (September 2001; www.whitehouse.gov/news. downloaded 6/18/07)

Bush's famous 2002 State of the Union address provides an additional example of the presence of the rogue image. In that speech, Bush identifies the "axis of evil:" Iraq, Iran, and North Korea as well as their "terrorist allies." These actors are described as follows:

> Some of these regimes have been pretty quiet since September the 11th. But we know their true nature. North Korea is a regime arming with missiles and weapons of mass destruction, while starving its citizens.
>
> Iran aggressively pursues these weapons and exports terror, while an unelected few repress the Iranian people's hope for freedom.
>
> Iraq continues to flaunt its hostility toward America and to support terror. The Iraqi regime has plotted to develop anthrax, and nerve gas, and nuclear weapons for over a decade. This is a regime that has already used poison gas to murder thousands of its own citizens—leaving the bodies of mothers huddled over their dead children. This is a regime that agreed to international inspections—then kicked out the inspectors. This is a regime that has something to hide from the civilized world. States like these, and their terrorist allies, constitute an axis of evil, arming to threaten the peace of the world. (January 29, 2002; www.whitehouse.gov/news. downloaded 6/6/07)

The statements are notable not because they accuse certain actors of doing bad things, but because of the dramatic simplification of each actor. They are very different regimes, lumped together in a single group, along with equally complex terrorist organizations. This illustrates the simplification that accompanies strong images, as images are meant to help easily and efficiently provide important information to the perceiver. There are vast assertions made about their motivations and capabilities together with these simplifications. They are described as indisputably threatening in their "true intentions," and they are repeatedly described as uncivilized. These characteristics all indicate a rogue image.

Another aspect of Bush's statement on Iraq in particular that indicates a rogue image is the instructive language used. In the mind of the perceiver, the rogue should be obedient. In Bush's mind, he and his administration make decisions, Saddam Hussein and the Iraqi military and the Iraqi people should follow those instructions. Indicative of such thinking, a March 17, 2003 speech by President Bush included the following:

> Saddam Hussein and his sons must leave Iraq within 48 hours. Their refusal to do so will result in military conflict commenced at a time of our choosing. Many Iraqis can hear me tonight in a translated radio broadcast, and I have a message for them: If we must begin a military campaign, it will be directed against the lawless men who rule your country and not against you. As our coalition takes away their power, we will deliver the food and medicine you need. We will tear down the apparatus of terror and we will help you to build a new Iraq that is prosperous and free. Your day of liberation is near. (www.cnn.worldnews. Downloaded 6/6/2007).

Earlier, in a March 6, 2003 press conference, Bush reiterated his perception of Saddam Hussein and his simplification of the politics and sectarian divisions in that country:

> Saddam Hussein has a long history of reckless aggression and terrible crimes. He possesses weapons of terror. He provides funding and training and safe haven to terrorists . . .
>
> America also accepts our responsibility to protect innocent lives in every way possible. We'll bring food and medicine to the Iraqi people. We'll help that nation to build a just government . . .
>
> The Iraqi people are plenty capable of governing themselves. . . . Iraq will provide a place where people can see that the Shia and the Sunni and the Kurds can get along in a federation.

President Bush closely followed the policy predisposition of those with a strong rogue image of another actor. There are indications that Bush planned to overthrow Saddam Hussein from the beginning of his first administration (*Seattle Post-Intelligencer*, January 4, 2004, A1). The decision-making history of President Bush and his administration regarding Iraq has been covered extensively by others (e.g., Woodward, 2006). Rather than review those events in great detail here, we offer instead illustrations of several crucial instances of the impact of the rogue image on decision making and information processing as the war plans developed.

The first of these instances is the administration's determination that Iraq had weapons of mass destruction (WMD) and intended to use them. In 2002 the CIA was asked to compose a National Intelligence Estimate on WMD in Iraq. According the then CIA director George Tenet, the NIE was done hurriedly, but still contained numerous reservations on the quality of the information about the Iraqi program (Tenet, 2007). He argues that uncertainty about the data was clear in the NIE (although not quite so clear in the summary), and that alternative views were made clear as well. Bush accepted the information that conformed with his preexisting image of Iraq's regime, that they had WMD and that they were going to use them. Given his image of Iraq and his dislike of details, this was a predictable outcome. Moreover, there was considerable pressure from those in the administration who shared this image to take indications that Iraq had or would soon have WMD to the neglect of contrary information (Risen, 2006).

One could argue that Bush was not the only one to make the mistake of taking as absolute fact the information that supported a preexisting image of Saddam Hussein. The FBI director George Tenet (2007) writes that he did too—most people thought Saddam at least had a program, and probably had some hidden weapons. However, a second decision-making and information-processing case that was used to push for public and Congressional support for the war was the alleged link between Saddam Hussein's regime and al-Qaeda. Tenet maintains that he insisted to Bush that there was no evidence of such a link (2007: 342), and the CIA's report indicated only that there were three areas of concern: that Iraq might provide safe havens, training, and/or intelligence for terrorist organizations. Nevertheless, Bush repeatedly asserted an Iraqi connection with al Qaeda and the 9/11 attacks on numerous occasions. He asserted that Saddam Hussein had contacts with al Qaeda going back over a decade and that Iraq "could decide on any given day to provide a biological or chemical weapon to a terrorist group or individual terrorists" (quoted in Isikoff & Corn, 2006: 146). Tenet also warned against stating that Iraq had been "caught" trying to purchase 500 tons of uranium oxide in Africa, but Bush did so in his 2003 State of the Union Address. Of course, the details of this particular case are in dispute. Tenet claims Assistant National Security Advisor Steven Hadley was told three months earlier, before Bush gave a speech in Cincinnati, that the accusation could not be made. After the State of the Union speech, Tenet was accused by National Security Advisor Condoleeza Rice and others for having failed to inform them that the intelligence did not support the accusation (Woodward, 2006). But this speaks once again to Bush's willingness to make statements using information that supported his preexisting views and to fail to verify for himself the details on which his policy was based.

So certain was Bush that Iraq had WMD, that days after he declared victory in Iraq, he stated in an interview with a Polish reporter, "We found the weapons of mass destruction. . . . We found biological laboratories. You remember when Colin Powell stood up in front of the world, and he said, Iraq has got laboratories, mobile labs to build the biological weapons. They're illegal. They're against the United Nations resolutions, and so far we've discovered two. And we'll find more weapons as time goes on. But for those who say we haven't found the banned manufacturing devices or banned weapons, they're wrong. We found them" (quoted in Woodward, 2006: 209–210). Of course, they had not found any weapons, but thinking they did conformed to his rogue image.

Another important illustration of the impact of the rogue image on the use of information, or failure to attend to information, was the administration's refusal to take seriously the State Department's study of Iraq, entitled The Future of Iraq Project. Congress authorized $5 million for a study of a postwar Iraq and the State Department produced a 2,500-page report with numerous recommendations for Iraq after the war was over, from political issues to matters as mundane but important as keeping electricity and water working. Secretary of Defense Rumsfeld discounted the report and, on orders from either Bush or Vice President Cheney, ordered that members of the team that composed the report be removed from the Pentagon team, led by Jay Garner, whose responsibility postwar Iraq would be (Woodward, 2006).[2] The complexities the report offered about the future of Iraq did not conform to the highly simplified image operative among the core decision makers of the administration.

The consequences of shutting out the State Department and its experts were considerable. Retired General Jay Garner was given the job of leading the reconstruction of Iraq by the Pentagon and he attempted to bring Thomas Warrick, who had led the State Department team in the postwar Iraq study, onto his team. However, Gerner was told by Rumsfeld (who implied the order came from Cheney) to fire Warrick. The efforts to marginalize the Warrick study meant Garner had to start essentially from scratch in terms of postwar planning. Garner had just eight weeks to develop a plan for stabilizing the situation on the ground for the Iraqis. As will be seen, the paucity in postwar planning and attention to the details of the complexities of Iraq would have grave consequences for the tribes of al Anbar and the US forces operating in the Sunni area. As a result of this shortened timeframe and exclusion of the DOS study, the Office of Reconstruction and Humanitarian Assistance (ORHA) was established in the Defense Department, under General Garner, on January 20, 2003. The office was started lacking Arab specialists, Arabic speakers, and other experienced specialists in postconflict recovery. Our accounts detailed here will highlight how the absence of specialists would impact future events in al Anbar.

The typical response to the perception of a rogue "misbehaving" is quick and stern punishment, conditions permitting. In this particular case, this was manifested in Bush and his administration's refusal to allow additional time for sanctions, inspections, negotiations, and a refusal for accommodation of the UN and NATO allies who strongly disagreed with his march to war. The simplifications of reality provided by strong images meant analysis absent consideration of complexities and context. Without these contextual cues for understanding behavior, along with a perception of weakness, low regard for Iraqi culture, and heightened threat perception, the initial behavioral predisposition associated with the rogue image is to quickly and unequivocally crush the rogue. This was the approach Bush and his administration took at various points regarding Iraq, and more specifically, the Sunnis in Iraq. According to Woodward (2006), Bush and his advisors saw the State Department, which constantly pushed for a more nuanced policy, as appeasers. Woodward quotes Richard Armitage as saying, "Their [the White House] idea of diplomacy is to say, 'Look fucker, you do what we want'" (2006: 329). Thus, Saddam Hussein was ordered to leave Iraq in 48 hours by Bush or face attack on March 17, 2003.

Administration policy makers also clashed with the military professionals regarding the size of the force necessary to overthrow the Iraqi regime. Again reflecting the rogue image (simple, childlike people with no political complexity), the administration, and particularly Rumsfeld and Wolfowitz, was certain that a relatively small force would be needed, because the Iraqis would welcome the Americans and the overthrow of Saddam Hussein. Given these perceptions, it was a logical conclusion that the construction of a new state would be straightforward as the Iraqis would henceforth follow instruction and leadership from the United States. As a result of these simplifications and lack of recognition of important Iraqi complexities, no importance was attributed to Iraqi nationalism, or the potential inflammation of sectarian conflict, which had been manipulated by Saddam to maintain his hold on power. Even such simple matters as the importance of postinvasion policing and the basic rule of law, and the possibility of simple criminal acts such as looting, were overlooked by the administration because of this pronounced tendency to simplify a complex reality through the prism of the rogue image. In this mindset, Americans were the good guys who will get rid of the rogue Saddam Hussein, be welcomed as liberators by a simplified and obedient public, and democracy will unfold under American tutelage.

One other vital and dire consequence to these simplifications was the assumption that postwar Iraq would not need a substantial US military force. The administration recommended a force of fewer than 100,000 (Ferguson, 2008). Assistant Secretary of Defense Wolfowitz, for example, stated thus, "'Our principal target is the psychological one, to convince the Iraqi people that they no longer have to be afraid of Saddam. . . . And once that happens I think what you're going to find, and this is very important, you're going to find Iraqis out cheering American troops. I am reasonably certain that they will greet us as liberators and that will help us keep the requirement down" (quoted in Ricks, 2006: 96, 97). Vice president Cheney made similar statements (Woodward, 2006). So convinced were they that the Iraqis would welcome the US forces, they believed that American troops would be withdrawn in three to four months (Ferguson, 2008). These types of simplifications of reality are more likely to occur when images are strongly held and regard for nuance and complexities is low because of a lack of appreciation for the culture and complexities of a perceived group, and a low opinion of the nature of the members of the group, in this case a rogue population led by a small elite.

However, Army Chief of Staff Eric Shinseki disagreed with this simplifications and their attendant optimism. Shinseki famously told Congress that he believed that several hundred thousand soldiers would be needed in Iraq for postwar peacekeeping. In testimony before the Senate Armed Forces Committee, he stated:

> I would say . . . something on the order of several hundred thousand soldiers . . . would be required. We're talking about post-hostilities control over a piece of geography that's fairly significant, with the kinds of ethnic tensions that could lead to other problems. And so it takes a significant ground-force presence. (quoted in Spain, 2012: 145)

The administration's response was delivered by Paul Wolfowitz, who told the House Budget Committee:

> There has been a good deal of comment, some of it quite outlandish, about what our postwar requirements might be in Iraq. Some of the higher end predictions we have been hearing recently, such as the notion that it will take several hundred thousand U.S. troops to provide stability in post-Saddam Iraq, are wildly off the mark. It is hard to conceive that it would take more forces to provide stability in post-Saddam Iraq than it would take to conduct the war itself and to secure the surrender of Saddam's security forces and his army; hard to imagine. (quoted in Spain, 2012: 146)

Other military leaders shared Shinseki's viewpoint. As one four-star general stated in an interview with Thomas Ricks:

> There were concerns both before we crossed the line of departure and after. . . . There was a conscious cutting off of advice and concerns, so that the guy who ultimately had to make the decision, the president, didn't get the advice. Well before the troops crossed the line of departure . . . concern was raised about what would happen in the postwar period, how you would deal with this decapitated country. It was blown off. Concern about a long term occupation—that was discounted. The people around the president were so, frankly, intellectually arrogant. They *knew* that postwar Iraq would be easy and would be a catalyst for change around the Middle East. They were making simplistic assumptions and refused to put them to the test. It's the vice president, and the secretary of defense, with the knowledge of the chairman of the Joint Chiefs and the vice chairman. They did it because they already had the answer, and they wouldn't subject their hypothesis to examination. (quoted in Ricks, 2006: 99)

The civilians at the Pentagon won this battle, although the force size, 148,000, was larger than they wanted.

The consequences of too few troops in Iraq were staggering. It led to the failure to stop looting (American troops reportedly ignored it and had no guidance on how to handle it); the inability to close the borders with Syria and Jordan[3] (and the lack of an awareness that this would be a major problem during postwar reconstruction), thus letting insurgents, particularly those associated with al Qaeda, free access to Iraq; assigning training of police and military personnel to private contractors instead of the US military; an inability to mind detainees, leading to scandals such as Abu Ghraib; and excessive violence and cultural insensitivity by American troops, which added fuel to the insurgency (Ricks, 2006; Ferguson, 2008). (These issues will be discussed in greater detail below.) The military planners share some responsibility because they too had no plans for "Phase IV," a postoverthrow occupation. The commonly accepted scenario among civilian and military planners that the Iraqi people would welcome the US forces included the notion that they would also welcome a government made up of exiles, in particular Ahmad Chalabi, an Iraqi Shiite who was living outside of Iraq for most of his life, and who had great influence with the US government. This assumption reflects a vast simplification of the Iraqis and their national identity. It also was a gross simplification that had severe negative consequences for the group dynamics in Iraq, which play such a vital role in the governance of Iraq.

L. PAUL BREMER, THE COALITION PROVISIONAL AUTHORITY, AND DE-BA'ATHIFICATION

While the target of the rogue image before the invasion was Saddam Hussein, it quickly became evident that the postoverthrow rogue image in Iraq was applied to the Sunnis as a group inside Iraq. As noted previously, the strategic preference for confronting those in the rogue image is to crush them. This is what happened to the Sunnis in Iraq when they encountered the US forces or attempted to work with the occupation. Hashim calls the view of the Sunnis "Sunniphobia" and argues that many neoconservatives in the administration, think tanks, and the media had this attitude (Hashim, 2006: 280). He argues that "the US administration totally discounted the Sunni reaction to the destruction of the regime. Just as we believed that the Shi'a would rise joyfully to embrace us, we also thought that the Sunnis could be treated with disdain, discounted and swept aside with little in the way of adverse reaction" (p. 280). The actions of the Coalition Provisional Authority (CPA) once L. Paul Bremer took over in May, 2003, reflect this outlook. Subsequently, this hostility toward the Sunnis filtered "down into the CPA in Baghdad"

(Hashim, 2006: 280) and added to an increasingly unstable and volatile group dynamic between the CPA and Sunnis in Iraq.

Bremer was selected by President Bush to head the CPA. The CPA and Bremer replaced the Office of Reconstruction and Humanitarian Assistance and retired General Jay Garner. For a variety of reasons, Bremer was ill-suited to the demanding position to which he was appointed. While he had served as a career foreign service officer, as ambassador to the Netherlands, and as a counterterrorism expert, he had no background in the politics of the Middle East, did not speak Arabic, and had no prior experience with postwar reconstruction (Ferguson, 2008). Bremer's limited expertise and background in the region prevented him from serving as a counterbalance to the administration's strong tendency to simplify complex realities in Iraq. In fact, his background likely amplified such tendencies. Bremer was given instructions before he went to Iraq to implement a policy of de-Ba'athification. In an insightful example of how the use of images can facilitate the use of poor analogies, Wolfowitz has been quoted stating that the Ba'athists were "Nazis" (Perry, 2010: 37) and Wolfowitz and others considered de-Ba'athification to be similar to de-Nazification in Germany after World War II. Bremer's opinion of the Sunnis in Iraq was simplistic, and reflected the rogue image just as strongly as the administration's tendency. This is hardly surprising, given the administration's tendency to exclude countering views from its inner circle advisory structure and therefore the decision-making process regarding Iraq. One telling example of the image held by Bremer is him telling one sheikh, Jaba Awad, "Every Sunni is a Ba'athist, every Ba'athist is a Saddamist, and every Saddamist is a Nazi" (quoted in Perry, 2010: 37).

This type of cognitive simplicity depoliticizes important behaviors and dynamics in Iraq and removes the critical group relationships from a context that provide any meaningful understandings of what is needed in a successful reconstruction and peace-building effort. The de-Ba'athification plan presented a particularly serious threat to Sunni identity that would echo throughout al Anbar with profound consequences. The plan appears in all of the interviews conducted of Sunni tribal leaders by our research team as a central event in their telling of the unraveling of security in al Anbar and the appearance of the insurgency. As such a pivotal event in the history of the Awakening, it is worth detailing the history of the implementation of the plan. Before Bremer went to his post in Iraq, he met with Secretary of Defense Rumsfeld and Doug Feith. They told Bremer about the de-Ba'athification plan, and he maintained that it should not go into effect until he arrived in Iraq and could issue the order (Bremer, 2006). The de-Ba'athification process involved two orders. The first, issued on May 16, 2003, called for the firing of all Ba'ath party members in positions in the first four tiers of government (Regional Command, Branch, Section, and Group) and their permanent ban from employment in the public sector. Bremer recalls in his memoirs that this could be done on a case-by-case basis, making exceptions for those who joined the party because it was a necessity for employment in the public sector, and those who had committed no crimes. He expected no more than 20,000 to lose their jobs (Bremer, 2006).

Nevertheless, it was quickly apparent that there would be massive firings, and that this would severely damage the effort to rebuild the country. Those targeted included teachers, administrators, professionals in hospitals and universities (Robinson, 2008). It included anyone who worked for the state and was a member of the Ba'ath Party, even if only nominally. Given that the Iraqi economy was dominated by the state, and the state provided 60% of employment, a lot of people were destined to lose their jobs and security as a result of the de-Ba'athification plan. Additionally, many would lose their positions of prestige and respect in their society, and as our interviews indicate, these actions were also interpreted as part of a conspiracy by Shi'a groups and the United States to attack the Sunni groups.

The plan was not without its critics. Objections came from Garner, the CIA, and many military officers, but the decision was made and was essentially irreversible. Following the decision, Bremer then put Ahmed Chalabi, the Shi'a expat, in charge of the process, including making exceptions. In one instance, General David Petraeus, then in charge of the Mosul area, realized that the order would result in the firing of all university professors, thereby cancelling graduation for all of the students. He asked Bremer for permission to rehire the professors and to work to develop a reconciliation process wherein people could come and denounce the Ba'ath Party, thereby allowing Petraeus to vet them and weed out the true believers. Bremer agreed, but when Chalabi took over the Iraqi de-Ba'athification committee, he eliminated all such reconciliation commissions' recommendations (Robinson, 2008). Thus ended the idea of making exceptions for nominal Ba'ath party members. This would have a profound impact not only on Iraqi life in the every-day sense, but also in the perceptions of Sunni power relative to Shi'a power in the new political environment.

As negatively impactful as the first decree was in terms of Iraqi national life and the financial security of broad swaths of average Iraqis and the group dynamics within the country, an even more impactful decision for general security and stability was yet to come. The second decree, issued on May 23, 2003, dissolved the Iraqi Army, the Republican Guard, paramilitary organizations, the intelligence services, the Secret Police, the Ministry of Defense, Ministry of Information, and other organizations (Ferguson, 2008). Salaries were no longer to be paid to people in these former organizations, and all records and weapons were to be confiscated. A "termination" payment would be made for all but the highest-ranking members of the organizations.

The CPA announced that it would create a new Iraqi Army. The decree resulted in the termination of the employment of 500,000–800,000 people (Ferguson, 2008: 164). As in the case of Order #1, there were protests from American military officers and others, many of whom argued that it is not possible to rebuild an army from scratch in fewer than ten years; that the Iraqi Military had always been seen as a national professional organization, and therefore not part of Hussein's personal regime; and that firing these people would lead to very angry, unemployed men with extensive experience with weapons and military practices. Nevertheless, Bremer argued that the army had disintegrated after the American victory, thus could not be reconstituted, and that even if it could be reconstituted it was unlikely that the conscripts, who were mostly Shi'a, would agree to serve under the former Saddam-era officers, who were mostly Sunni (Bremer, 2006). In addition, there was no place to train a reconstituted army because their bases had been looted. This position regarding the training of the military was reiterated by Bremer's underling, Walter Slocombe, in an interview with Charles Ferguson (2008). In other interviews with "dozens" of people who were experts on the Middle East and Iraq, workers from the ORHA, the US military, journalists, and NGOs, Ferguson found that:

> According to the interviewees, many Iraqi army officers cared about the welfare of their men, and the army did not simply "dissolve," but rather heeded American promises and warnings that if the army cooperated and did not fight, it would be treated with respect after the war. The interviewees also said that recalling the army was both extremely important and eminently feasible and that plans for the recall were well under way when Bremer announced his order. (p. 171)

The interviewees also noted that the Iraqi Army had not disintegrated; they merely went home as it was clear that resisting the American assault would be futile. According to one interviewee, Joost Hiltermann, "they were very willing to be called up and to [come] back to the destroyed bases because there was still a command and control structure" (2008: 172). (As will be seen when we turn to the tribal perspective, they too were certain that the army could be reconstituted after the combat phase was over.) Other of Ferguson's interviewees maintained that the Iraqi Army did not have such a simple monolithic Ba'athist officer corps and Shi'a inductees. In fact, there were Sunnis and Shi'a at both levels in the preinvasion army (p. 175). Personnel records also confirmed that the officers were not all Ba'ath Party members. The records showed that only half of the officers at the rank of General were Ba'athists, and lower level officers were less than a majority Baasthists, but Slocombe maintained that anyone above the rank of colonel would be ineligible for membership in a new Iraqi Army because they were all Ba'athists (p. 176).

Again, both of these orders had ample opposition. According to Deputy Secretary of State Richard Armitage, as well as Jay Garner and others, both President Bush and the National Security Council understood de-Ba'athification to have a much more limited scope than that implemented under Order #1 (Ricks, 2006; Ferguson, 2008). Based on these accounts, the historical record indicates these decisions and the interpretations of them were largely done by Rumsfeld, Wolfowitz, Feith, Bremer, and Slocombe. Similarly, the US military had planned to and were working with elements of the Iraqi Army to try to rebuild it. This was an explicit part of the Phase IV plan, called Eclipse II, with the assumption that "there would be large numbers of Iraqi security forces willing and able to support the occupation" (from the Army War College summary quoted in Ricks, 2006: 110). CentCom made plans for their recruitment as well.[4] Some American officers reported having over 130,000 soldiers from the Iraqi Army signed up (Ferguson, 2008). As in the case of Order #1, Richard Armitage recalled that the plan discussed at the NSC was to "disband echelons above battalion and keep battalion below as a force to be utilized, to provide security, et cetera" (quoted in Ferguson, 2008: 217). As in the case of Order #1, the decision on Order #2 was made by Bremer, on the advice of Slocombe, and approved by Rumsfeld (Ferguson, 2008; Bremer, 2006).

The end result of the expansive de-Ba'athification program was a burgeoning insurgency by late fall, 2003, and early winter 2004. In addition to firing the people who knew how to keep the country running, with water, electricity, and health care, the deposed army members felt betrayed. The United States had dropped fliers as the war commenced, urging them to lay down their arms and offering the reward for doing so of being made part of a postwar Iraqi army. Instead they lost their jobs, their dignity, their income, and their future prospects. They took their weapons with them when they went home, they were trained, and they were good candidates for an insurgency in terms of training and motivation.

Finally, Bremer turned the intervention into an occupation. The initial intention had been to move quickly to have an interim Iraqi government installed, but Bremer and Rumsfeld decided not to move in that direction, and cancelled upcoming local elections in Iraq. The CPA became the governing authority in Iraq. Bremer did create an Iraqi Interim Governing Council, but it had no real power. It was led and appointed by Bremer and its seats were allocated through sectarian-based quotas (Ferguson, 2008). The Council lasted until June, 2004, when Ayad Allawi was named prime minister of an interim government, to be replaced through elections in January 2005.

THE US MILITARY: MISTAKES, REGRETS, AND EARLY CORRECTIONS

While the civilians at the CPA had an unrelenting boss in L. Paul Bremer, the US military's approach to the postwar complex of problems in Iraq had significant deficiencies and they made a number of mistakes, including not having counterinsurgency plans and training, and rough treatment of civilians. There was conflict between military officials and civilian DoD decision makers. As was mentioned, from the outset of planning for the war, force levels were a problem. Many in the military high command wanted a force level much higher than the civilian planners in the Pentagon advocated (Ricks, 2006). Those same civilians did not plan for a postinvasion force: They disdained nation building and wanted the Iraqis to "solve their own problems" (Robinson, 2008: 20) once the United States had disposed of Saddam Hussein's regime. While the civilian planners had no interest in, and anticipated no need for, a large American presence in postwar Iraq, the Army, in a parallel fashion, had developed an approach to war that added to the potential for postwar problems. Lt. Col. Antulio Echeverria argues that since Desert Storm and its success, the military had come to believe in airpower and tank-based assaults, with minimal casualties, and battle-centered war scenarios with quick and precise assaults on the enemy's "centers of gravity," thereby paralyzing the enemy and providing victory (2004: 8). This leads to a "way of war" that is actually a way of battle, and that fails to see the overall purpose of the war as the strategic goal. Thus, in Iraq, it was the battle for Baghdad rather than the Iraq War that was the centerpiece of US strategic thinking. That part of the war ended quickly and smoothly as the regime crumbled under the onslaught of American firepower. In accordance with the military's approach to war, the plan for postwar operations, Eclipse II, was based on three weak assumptions; that Iraqi security forces would step in after the regime was overthrown to provide security for the populace; that other countries would join in to assist postwar stability; and that a new Iraqi government would be formed quickly and to the satisfaction of the Iraqis (Ricks, 2006: 110).

None of these things came to pass, and the military, like the civilians in OSD, had no effective postwar plan and no basis for anticipating the growth of a powerful and hostile insurgency. Indeed, counterinsurgency as a concept was tainted with the failure of Vietnam with which counterinsurgency was associated by many. Vietnam, like Iraq, involved conventional and counterinsurgency warfare. However, by the 1990s, "counterinsurgency was a musty corner of the American military" (Maass, 2004). Soldiers received some training in it, but, as one former Lt. Colonel in the army put it, "it was back burner and we didn't think too much about it" (personal communication

2/26/2014). Soldiers were generally trained to fight and kill the enemy, not to worry about the "hearts and minds" of the civilians (Ricks, 2006; Packer, 2005). The Pentagon referred to counterinsurgency as "military operations other than war." As will be seen below, a number of individual officers understood early on the importance of having good relations with the civilian Iraqi population, but the idea that an insurgency was possible or actually occurring was unacceptable to the American civilian leadership.

This approach to war had a number of important results. First, the military was unprepared for the lawlessness and looting that occurred after the regime was overthrown. Soldiers reportedly stood by watching looters in action, making no attempt to stop them. This made the United States appear ineffective, confused, and uncaring (Ricks, 2006). Second, because of the size of the American force, and the operating assumption that there would be no insurgency, the borders with Syria, Jordan, and Saudi Arabia were not protected. Indeed, given the force size, the task of trying to control the borders was simply impossible. The borders ultimately became a sieve through which foreign insurgents flowed. Third, expecting the Iraqi security forces to step back up after the regime was overthrown, there was no military anticipation of de-Ba'athification. In fact, there was a significant amount of hostility and lack of communication between Bremer and the CPA and General Ricardo Sanchez and the military (Ferguson, 2008). De-Ba'athification made the reemergence of the Iraqi security forces impossible, and as a result someone had to train a new police force and army. The US military was unprepared for this, and hired private contractors such as DynCorp to do the job (Robinson, 2008). The lack of military preparedness to train a new police force is particularly ironic. It is an important illustration of both the failure to bring a large enough force size and failure to anticipate the difficulties of providing stability after the war. Retired Colonel Ted Spain, Commander of the 18th Military Police Brigade when American forces went into Iraq, has described the difficulties they faced trying to train a new police force and deal with detainees in *Breaking Iraq* (2012). Spain explains that the MPs entered Iraq without the force size they needed. They were unable to provide security for the convoys entering Iraq as the war started, and they were unable to provide security for the Iraqi people after the regime fell. In addition, he had to act repeatedly, and not always successfully, to make sure the MPs were used as MPs, not as combat soldiers, when assigned to combat units. There was also little guidance on how to evaluate detainees (e.g., how to determine if one is a terrorist, criminal, or enemy combatant) and where to put them both as they were captured during the invasion and later in prisons.

A fourth, and very serious, consequence of the US military's general approach to war goes back to the lack of a counterinsurgency plan. The military varied considerably in the way it treated Iraqi civilians. Given that the training focused on destroying the enemy, this is not surprising. Generally, "senior U.S. commanders tried to counter the insurgency with indiscriminate cordon-and-sweep operations that involved detaining thousands of Iraqis" (Ricks, 2006: 195). Many of the detainees ended up in prisons like Abu Ghraib, where they were mistreated and abused by poorly trained and supervised military guards and civilian contractors. Others were abused while detained on US bases. The 4th Infantry Division, under Major General Ray Odierno, had a reputation of being extremely aggressive in its treatment of the civilian population. Night raids on homes, breaking down doors, tossing people's belongings, arresting people, roughing people up, and humiliating them were common tactics. As will be seen when we turn to the Iraqi perspective, this approach added fuel to the insurgency. As the insurgency blossomed in May and June, 2003, it was dismissed in a manner entirely consistent with the rogue image. Very low regard was given to the causes of the insurgents' grievances, or their standing in society. The insurgents were dismissed and considered "dead-enders" of the previous regime. Deputy Secretary of Defense Paul Wolfowitz announced at the end of June, 2003, while the insurgency was growing, that "The direction is pretty clear. It is toward a more secure Iraq. . . . [The insurgents] lack the sympathy of the population, and they lack any serious external support, Basically, they are on their own" (quoted in Hashim, 2006: 59). Defense Secretary Donald Rumsfeld agreed, stating in July 2003, "I guess the reason I don't use the phrase 'guerrilla war' is because there isn't one" (quoted in Packer, 2005: 302).

Others, such as then-Major General Petraeus, who commanded the 101st Airborne Division in the Mosul area, and Marine Lt. General James Conway, Commander of the 1st Marine Expeditionary Force (1-MEF) in the Fallujah area, were more inclined to use methods to get the population on their side such as more judicious uses of force, and attention to economic needs and security. Both were concerned with building trust among the Iraqis. This pattern among American military leaders is important in understanding the Awakening movement and the future cooperation with American forces. While the military as a whole did not adopt a formal counterinsurgency doctrine until Petraeus took command of the Multi-National Force-Iraq (MNF-I) in January 2007, individual leaders such as Conway, Petraeus, Major John Nagl, and then-Colonel H.R. McMaster studied and implemented counterinsurgency methods that helped facilitate a broader shift in strategy and a shift in perceptions. General Casey, who succeeded General Sanchez, also had an interest in using more counterinsurgency tactics in the face of the rising insecurity in Iraq.

The variance in the tactics used, and the general tendency in the army to use aggressive and violent tactics against the Iraqi populace, is reflective of poor coordination as well as the lack of a counterinsurgency approach to war, particularly in 2003–2004. It is also yet another indication of the image of a rogue, an actor best dealt with by the use of force as an attempt to punish and discipline the misbehavior. Lt. General Sanchez has since come under considerable criticism for exercising inadequate leadership. One Army intelligence officer is quoted by Ricks stating, "For the first year of the war . . . there was no campaign plan issued to military personnel" by Sanchez's command to respond to either the growing insurgency or reconstruction needs (2006: 226). Sanchez apparently did not grasp, or failed to convey effectively, the importance of the relationship between US military actions and political outcomes. Consequently, different field commanders used different tactics, and there was little coordination, or, as Ricks puts it, "each sector felt like a separate war, with different approaches and rules, showing a lack of coordination that runs against the repeated findings of theorists and practitioners of counterinsurgency" (2006: 226). The difference in tactics is described by then-Lt. General Conway, the commander of 1-MEF in 2004 in al Anbar, who recalled clashes with General Sanchez:

> We were paying particular concern to the northern Babil Province. It was probably the most hostile of all the areas that we owned south of Baghdad. And on one occasion, [General Sanchez] wanted to completely change our method of operations and have us sweep through the province. On another occasion, he wanted to sign over the province, or that portion of the province, for a period of time and let the 1st Airborne roll tanks and tracks through there for a period of two weeks and then give it back to us. And we said no, those things are absolutely not going to happen. (Conway, Marine interview 2009 V.1: 45)

The importance of the position taken by different commanders cannot be underestimated. The army did not have a counterinsurgency plan, and even the Marines, which tended to have more of "small wars" mission than the army, did not have a counterinsurgency program (Packer, 2005). Moreover, officers were punished for suggesting that they were not prepared for the enemies they began to encounter. General William Wallace, for example, stated, "The enemy we're fighting is a bit different from the one we war-gamed against" in a *New York Times* interview in April 2003 (quoted in Spain, 2012: 144). According to Spain (2012), Secretary of Defense Rumsfeld, General Richard Myers, and General Tommy Franks became "unhinged at the comments Wallace made" (p. 145).

One result of the lack of preparation for an insurgency at both the military and the civilian levels was an inadequate capacity to gather intelligence as the insurgency grew in 2003. On a larger and more fundamental scale, however, they failed to anticipate the probability of an insurgency. If they had, they would have also anticipated that the best way to prevent an insurgency is to make the populace secure, and to give them a reason to give new governing structures a chance to work. But the first order of business after de-Ba'athificatiion was the development of a new Iraqi Army, rather than the police, the latter being the best suited of the two to provide security for the average citizen. In terms of the training of a new Army, the Pentagon handed that job over to the CPA, which in turn hired a private contractor, Vinnell, to do it. With a contract worth $48 million, Vinnel was supposed to train twenty-two battalions, but only trained six, and half of those soldiers deserted (Packer, 2005: 306).

Abu Ghraib

In May, 2003, MP commander Colonel Ted Spain discovered Abu Ghraib, a prison outside of Baghdad that had been badly damaged during the invasion (Spain, 2013). Having a facility to house prisoners captured by American forces was of great importance and the decision was made to refurbish Abu Ghraib since building a new prison from scratch would take a great deal of time. While work was being done on the prison, several hundred detainees were already confined to the prison (Spain, 2013). Brigadier General Janis Karpinski took over responsibility for Abu Ghraib and other prisons on June 20, 2003, as the commander of the 800th MP Brigade. Karpinsky was an Army reserve officer with no experience in running a prison. The prison officially opened on August 4, 2003, and was called the Baghdad Central Correctional Facility (McKelvey, 2007). In October, 2003, the 372nd Military Police Company, which was an Army Reserve company, took over Tiers 1A and 1B (Ricks, 2006). These tiers housed detainees who were believed to have valuable information. Less important detainees were housed in tents in outdoor areas of the prison.

In the days that followed, prisoners were tortured, raped, sodomized, abused, humiliated, and photographed in their misery. On November 20, army teams with dogs arrived at the prison, and the dogs were subsequently used to further abuse the prisoners (Ricks, 2006). The abuse was reported to military authorities sometime in December, 2003, or January, 2004, when Specialist Joseph Darby gave a military investigator a CD with photographs of the abuse (McKelvey, 2007). The pictures and the investigation into the abuses were made public in April, 2004. The ensuing scandal was very damaging for perceptions of Americans in Iraq and across the Middle East, as well as among the American public. As Tony Karon reported at the time:

> Days before the first photographs of detainee abuse appeared on CBS, a CNN/USA Today Gallup poll found that 60 percent of Iraqis now want U.S. troops to go home immediately, even though they acknowledge that their departure might bring further instability. Those numbers captured a decisive swing

> away from the U.S. in the mood of Iraqis over the year since Saddam Hussein's regime fell. . . . It's a safe bet that in the wake of the mass circulation of the Abu Ghraib photographs across all media platforms in the Arab world, the number of Iraqis wanting an immediate U.S. withdrawal will almost certainly have increased. (downloaded from http://content.time.com/time/world/article/0,8599,632967,00.html 5/11/2010)

The investigation that followed identified seventeen officers and soldiers, as well as a civilian contractor, as responsible, and recommended they be removed from duty. Eleven were convicted in the courts-martial that followed. The low-ranking soldiers who committed the abuse and the General responsible for Abu Ghraib, Karpinsky, received the official blame for the scandal, and deservedly so. However, there were multiple reasons this abuse took place, some of which have their origins in the basic lack of planning for the postinvasion chaos and growing insurgency, as well as de-Ba'athification. First, the MPs in the 372nd had no training guidelines for guarding prisoners. They had been traffic cops before being assigned to Abu Ghraib. Two of the most infamous abusers, Staff Sergeant Ivan Frederick and Specialist Charles Graner, were prison corrections officers in civilian life, and so were given leadership roles (Hersh, 2004). Frederick and his defense attorney argued that he was merely carrying out orders; that military intelligence, CIA officers, and civilian defense contractors specializing in interrogation wanted to break detainees by making them naked, putting women's undergarments on their heads, physically assaulting them, and frightening them with dogs (Hersh, 2004; Ricks, 2006). The decision to "take the gloves off" in interrogating prisoners was made in a memo sent on August 14, 2003, from General Sanchez's headquarters, and supported by the "Torture Memo" issued by the Justice Department in 2002 (Ricks, 2006; McKelvey, 2007). The Senate Armed Services Committeee eventually assigned responsibility for the abuses to Secretary of Defense Donald Rumsfeld (Scott & Mazzetti, 2008). In short, while several individuals were blamed for the abuse, the mistreatment was a widespread technique used by military intelligence and private contractor interrogators.

The focus on the individuals involved in the Abu Ghraib scandal diverts attention from the bigger picture. The American forces simply were not prepared for the chaos and the insurgency that followed the invasion. The Iraqi police were gone, a result of de-Ba'athification, so there were no culturally informed guards. The prison was receiving detainees before it was structurally renovated, so it was difficult to control the prisoners. By mid-May, 2003, as engineers started to work on the prison, the prison already held several hundred detainees, who charged the guards (Spain, 2013). In addition, it was difficult to identify detainees, which made their treatment uncertain. Colonel

Spain, the MP commander, wrote that in addition to Iraqi soldiers, the detainees included civilian noncombatants, members of al Qaeda, and Fedayeen soldiers from the Iraqi Army who used terrorist tactics (2013: 99–100). As time progressed, thousands of civilian Iraqis were arrested after their homes were raided, and they were hauled from their homes to places unknown to their families (Ricks, 2006). The demand for intelligence grew as the insurgency that the US planners had not anticipated grew. On August 31, 2003, Major General Geoffrey Miller, who was the commander of detainee treatment at Guantanamo Bay, arrived in Iraq to give advice. He advocated using the prisoner "softening" techniques used in Guantanamo in Iraq. He did not consider the differences in the two situations, with Guantanamo secure and remote, while prisons in Iraq were in a combat zone. In Guantanamo the ratio of prisoner to guard was 1 to 1, while in Iraq it was initially 1 guard to 10 prisoners, a ratio that quickly became much greater (Ricks, 2006). Miller's recommendations were written up in the "Assessment of DoD Counterterrorism Interrogation and Detention Operations in Iraq" report. In order to make interrogations more productive, he wrote the following:

> Recommendation: dedicate and train a detention guard force subordinate to the JIDC [Joint Interrogation and Debriefing Center] that sets the conditions for the successful interrogation and exploitation of internees/detainees. This action is now in progress. . . . It is essential that the guard force be actively engaged in setting the conditions for successful exploitation of the internees. (quoted in McKelvey, 2007: 11)

Karpinski claimed that Miller and Lieutenant General Sanchez took control of intelligence gathering at Abu Ghraib, and that Miller stated, "A detainee never leaves the cell if he's not escorted by two MPs in leg irons, and hand irons, and a belly chain. And there was no mistake about who was in charge. And you have to treat these detainees like dogs" (quoted in McKelvey, 2007: 12). The military investigation of the scandal was led by Major General Antonio Taguba. He believes that the MPs were "literally exploited by the military interrogators" and that General Ricardo Sanchez knew what was going on in Abu Ghraib (quoted in Hersh, 2007: 9).

As American forces met the growing insurgency with aggressive tactics against the civilian Iraqis, the number of prisoners increased rapidly. The prisoner population at Abu Ghraib went from 3,500 in September, 2003, to almost twice that by the next month (Ricks, 2006: 199). The prison was under constant attack and prisoners kept escaping. On November 24, 2003, the prisoners staged a riot. Nine were shot dead and nine Americans were injured (Ricks, 2006: 193). The prison had very little in terms of defensive capacity, only M-16s and squad automatic weapons (SAWs), and Karpinski complained that they were having unscreened prisoners dumped by hundreds (Ricks, 2006). Overall, the situation was a recipe for prisoner abuse, known as "monstering" (McKelvey, 2007).

Fallujah

The early insurgency can be attributed in part to the de-Ba'athification program that deprived Sunnis, in particular, of incomes, jobs, and political power. By the late spring and summer of 2003, the situation in Iraq was becoming increasingly violent. Events in Fallujah accelerated the spread of the insurgency in al Anbar Province. Fallujah, the second largest city in al Anbar Province, with 280,000 people, was known as the city of mosques because of the large number of mosques. It was very conservative, Salafist ideas had become popular among the young, and Sunni clerics held a great deal of political power in the city, more than tribal sheikhs. The city had prospered under Saddam Hussein, and although it was not particularly pro-Ba'athist, or anti-American initially, the de-Ba'athification program had serious negative economic consequences there. When the Americans were coming to Fallujah in April 2003, the young clerics warned that the Americans would turn the city over to the Shi'a, and Iraq over to Israel (West, 2006).

Fallujah was initially occupied by the Army's 82nd Airborne. They had several clashes with civilians, resulting in a number of civilian deaths. One incident that particularly riled the residents of Fallujah took place on April 28, 2003, when the Americans killed fifteen people and wounded sixty-five during an anti-US rally (Hashim, 2006: 23). The 82nd Airborne was replaced by the 3rd Armored Cavalry Regiment and the 101st Airborne Division in May 2003, but returned to Fallujah in September, 2003.

The 82nd Airborne did have a goal of winning over the local population. Initially, the commander, Major General Charles Swannack, estimated that only one percent of the populace was inclined to actively resist the American forces (Baram, 2005). The 82nd Airborne tried to target only insurgents, and to prevent the deaths of innocents. They also tried to provide employment for as many men as possible, including 2,200 Iraqi border guards, and they used $41 million for civic improvement and other employment opportunities (Baram, 2005). However, they did engage in numerous exchanges as Fallujah became increasingly violent, and when this happened they used aggressive tactics (West, 2006). In April, 2003, US soldiers opened fire on a crowd of demonstrators, believing mistakenly that there were snipers present, and killed sixteen innocent civilians. As fighting escalated in the fall of 2003, Major General Swannack authorized Operation Iron Hammer, saying, "This is war. . . . I am going to use a sledgehammer to crush a walnut" (quoted in West, 2006: 34).

On March 24, 2004, Lt. General Conway's 1-MEF took over in Fallujah. They were spread across the Province of al Anbar. Conway and the commander of the 1st Marine Division (under Conway), Major General Mattis, believed that the Americans could not defeat an insurgency without Iraqi help, and that they needed to show respect for the populace (Perry, 2010). As Mattis wrote to his troops, "The enemy will try to manipulate you into hating all Iraqis. . . . Do not allow the enemy that victory. With strong discipline, solid faith, unwavering alertness, and undiminished chivalry for the innocent, we will carry out this mission. Remember, I have added 'First, Do No Harm' to our passwords of 'No Better Friend, No Worse Enemy.'" (quoted in West, 2006: 50).

As the Marine commanders prepared for redeployment to Iraq, they identified three groups of potential opponents in al Anbar. According to Major General Mattis, these were "the tribes, there were criminals amongst them, and what we thought we needed for them was jobs and securing them, the locals. Then we had the former regime elements. These were the recalcitrant ones, the ones who chose to be irreconcilable. There were criminals amongst them, too. And then we had the foreign fighters, not many, when you ran into them, because you generally didn't take prisoners. They fought to the death" (Marine interview I, 2009: 23–24). They went in with a clear counterinsurgency doctrine (COIN) according to Mattis, and knew that they had to give the tribes priority, recognizing their political importance. Moreover, they understood that a large American presence in the city of Fallujah would be resented. They planned to use intelligence for Special Forces operations to go in and get suspected insurgents (Mattis Marine interview: 27)

Although the Marines recognized that their presence in Fallujah antagonized the residents, they did conduct patrols upon arriving there and the patrols were involved in a number of firefights that resulted in fifteen dead Iraqis (Ricks, 2006: 331). Then on March 31, four employees of Blackwater Security went into Fallujah without informing the Marines. Their travel plans were leaked and they were met with an ambush near the center of town. The four were beaten, killed, dismembered, and two of the bodies (or parts of them) were hung from a bridge known as Brooklyn Bridge with a cheering mob looking on. General Conway was ordered to attack and punish the insurgents on April 3, 2004. Top leadership, from President Bush through Secretary of Defense Rumsfeld, to L. Paul Bremer and Lt. General Sanchez, wanted a strong response. General Conway reportedly was furious that he was being ordered to send Marines into Fallujah without a carefully constructed plan of attack. He also believed it would backfire and make more enemies for the Marines (Perry, 2010). General Conway later remarked that his preference would have been to "let the situation settle before we appeared to be attacking out of revenge" (Chandrasekaran, 2004: A17). General Mattis concurred, and recalls that he said to General Conway, "I don't want to go into the city," to which Conway replied, "That's exactly what the enemy wants us to do right now. We will continue the operations around the periphery of the city" (Mattis, Marine Interview, 2009 V1: 34).

Rather than attack the city, the Marine preference was to find the individuals responsible for the killings. As Bing West notes, "Before they attacked, key Iraqi officials and allies had to be informed and brought on board. And once the Marines seized the city, someone had to administer municipal services—electricity, water, traffic movement. That meant insuring Iraqis supported the attack. The strategic groundwork hadn't been prepared" (2006: 59). Moreover, there was no strategic plan specifying what was to be accomplished by attacking Fallujah.

Objections aside, the Marines were ordered to attack, and on April 2 they cordoned off the city. Checkpoints were established, and on April 4 they cut off the city. Operation Vigilant Resolve commenced with very fierce street fighting on April 5. In response, fighting spread throughout Iraq, but particularly in Ramadi, the capital of al Anbar Province. Within a few days, complaints were pouring in over the destruction and deaths in Fallujah. Several members of the Iraqi Governing Council in Baghdad quit and others denounced the military campaigns as "unacceptable" and "illegal" (West, 2006: 119). On April 9, the Marines were ordered to cease-fire, having taken between a quarter to a third of the city (Perry, 2010; West, 2006; Conway interview 2009: 50). It was estimated that six hundred Iraqis, civilians and insurgents, had been killed.

Following the cease-fire, confusion abounded as to who had what authority to take the next steps. There was disagreement about the cease-fire and whether the attack should resume. Meanwhile, one option Conway considered was the formation of a local Iraqi military force using former Iraqi army officers in Fallujah. This option was rejected by the CPA representative at the MEF, since it would amount to bringing Ba'athists back into power (West, 2006). Nevertheless, Conway formed the "Fallujah Brigade," which was supposed to be composed of former Iraqi generals who would recruit soldiers from the old Iraqi army and turn insurgents in Fallujah into members of the Fallujah Brigade (Chandrasekaran, 2004; West, 2006). The Marines would provide money and weapons. They initially attempted to include joint patrols with Marines and Iraqis, but that idea never got off the negotiating table. The Fallujah Brigade soldiers were supposed to wear desert camouflage uniforms, confiscate insurgents' weapons, restore order, and man traffic checkpoints into the city. Meanwhile, American forces would withdraw from the city.

The decision-making process in this case is interesting, and it illustrates the growing separation between the US military and the civilian diplomatic arm in the CPA. When Bremer found out about the agreement to form the Fallujah Brigade he was angry, and he had not been informed about or involved in the negotiations (Bremer, 2006). Instead, Lt. General Conway had asked for permission from his superiors to proceed: Lt. Generals John Abizaid (Army, CentCom Commander) and Ricardo Sanchez (Army, senior US Commander in Iraq). Lt. General Sanchez did not inform Bremer, and Lt General Conway did not inform the CPA authorities in al Anbar. Lt. General Abizaid did not inform or consult with Washington. It is one of the first major instances of military authorities making decisions that had the political goal of turning Iraq back to Iraqi control. In this case, unfortunately, it did not work. It quickly became apparent that the Fallujah Brigade was not taking down the insurgency but letting it build up. Fallujah became a home for the insurgency. By September, Iraqi prime minister Ayad Allawi[5] disbanded the Brigade. Needless to say, this did not eliminate the insurgency. Fighting continued between the Marines and the insurgents.

Finally, on November 8, 2004, US, British, and Iraqi forces launched Operation Al-Fajr ("the dawn" in Arabic, and the name preferred by Prime Minister Allawi)/Operation Phantom Fury to clear the insurgents out of Fallujah. It lasted until December 23, when the last of the insurgents were wiped out. It is considered the bloodiest battle of the Iraq war, and was well planned for. By then General George Casey Jr. had replaced Lt. General Sanchez, and initiated an effort to develop a coherent campaign, which Lt. General Sanchez never did. The plan called for "containing the insurgent violence, building up Iraqi security forces, rebuilding economically, and reaching out to the Sunni community through both coercion and cooptation" (Ricks, 2006: 393). Casey began the new focus on counterinsurgency, but the devil was always in the details. They never thought through how the protection of the population would be done, particularly in the long term, and how it would all end (Whiteside, 2015, personal correspondence).

Ramadi

By this time the insurgency spread across al Anbar and it was zooming in on the provincial capital in Ramadi. The governor in 2004 was Kareem Burgis, who was well regarded by the American military there. Burgis had three children who were kidnapped by insurgents. He was forced to resign and make an anti-American statement in order to get his family back from the insurgents. He later fled with his family to Jordan. The Province experienced a period of political upheaval at the time following Burgis's resignation, and it went through a succession of governors after Burgis's departure: Faisal al Gaood was appointed in November 2004, but resigned after six months for another position; then came Raja Nawaf Farhan al Mahalawi, who was assassinated;

and then Mamoun Sami Rashid al Alwani, a member of the Islamic Party of Iraq. The insurgents in Ramadi ultimately took control of much of the city in the midst of the political turmoil.

NOTES

1. It is an exaggeration to state that the insurgency started in al Anbar. There were earlier attacks by nationalist insurgents including sniping, assassinations, and IEDs in Baghdad and elsewhere. The authors thank Craig Whiteside for this point.

2. Other factors in addition to the political psychology factors affecting this development are the strong personal clashes between Secretary of Defense Rumsfeld and Secretary of State Powell, as well as bureaucratic competition between the Office of the Secretary of Defense and the State Department for control of the Iraq policy. That the State Department would lose was essentially a given when on January 20, 2003, President Bush signed National Security Presidential Directive 24, giving the Pentagon control of postwar Iraq (Ferguson, 2008).

3. Shutting the borders would probably have been impossible. The point is that there was no top-level recognition that serious efforts to control those borders were called for.

4. Some of Ferguson's interviewees, such as Colonel James Torgler, believed that Bremer and Slocombe did not know the difference between the Iraqi Army, which was nationalist and professional, and the Republican Guard, who were hardcore Saddam loyalists and thugs.

5. Iraq returned to Iraqis at the end of June 2004, an interim government was appointed, and the CPA was dissolved.

Chapter 3

The Tribes

High Expectations and Disappointment

Details on the nature of tribal interaction and the interests of the sheikhs were provided in Chapter 1. Here we begin an analysis of the Sunni tribes in al Anbar Province as they anticipated the invasion by the United States and its allies. The Sunni tribes in al Anbar had survived the Saddam Hussein years, but the regime took its toll on the tribes. Some of the sheikhs fled Iraq, including the sheikh of sheikhs, Sheikh Majed. In the resulting vacuum, "fake sheikhs" loyal to Saddam Hussein emerged. Once it was clear that the United States intended to intervene in Iraq, the real sheikhs prepared to return and participate in Sunni and Iraqi political life. They also fully intended to take advantage of the end of the regime, to the benefit of their tribes, and this meant interacting early on with the Americans. Below we see present the financial and identity-based motivations, and also the roots of disappointment as a result of their treatment at the hands of the Americans, who had increasingly viewed them, the Sunni tribes, as rogues.

The tribal sheikhs' general image of the United States was of the imperialist. That image is complicated in the sense that the imperialist has both beneficial and harmful characteristics. It is seen as having more capability than the perceiver, and is exploitive in intentions. However, imperial powers are also associated with a history in which they would select a section of a colonial society to serve as their local administrators, and therefore the beneficiaries of any imperial largesse. The local elite would have more power than any other sector of society. The Iraqis were familiar with this since it was the pattern followed by the British during their imperial reign in Iraq. The local elite chosen by the British were the Sunnis, and the Sunni tribes in al Anbar assumed, based on this history, that this would be repeated in the upcoming invasion and likely occupation. Consequently, the form of the imperial image they held was the benevolent form. They expected the United

States to overthrow Saddam Hussein, put them in charge, and form a new Iraq. As Sheikh Aakab al Gaood put it, "We know that the goal of American forces in Iraq was to liberate Iraq. After 2003, most of the people thought positively of the liberators" (Interview 3/15/2010). Staff Brigadier General Haqi Isma'eel Ali Hameed concurred, saying:

> Before the invasion . . . the people of Iraq expected something different than what they actually saw after the operation. Everyone thought there would be democracy and an improvement in the scientific and technological fields, and the quality of life would improve. They thought that all of this would happen after the operation.
>
> After the invasion of Iraq by the Coalition forces, and after they were inside all the cities and towns, we saw some really strange and weird behavior by the Coalition forces, especially what they did with honest Iraqis who were unarmed. (Marine interview 2009: 221)

Sheikh Tariq also held this view:

> I remember very well that the people were very happy about this change [Saddam's overthrow], they accept that the Americans remove the regime and replace them with other people. Everyone was prepared that the Americans would come with a solution, they would come with educated Iraqi people to replace, to take over the situation. (Interview 3/10/2010)

Recognition of the superior capability and dominating culture associated with the imperial image is also evident in comments made by Iraqis. This is reflected in General Ra'ad Hamdani's (commander of the II Republican Guard Corps under Saddam Hussein) interview during which he stated:

> My view that countries like the US, they are countries, or states, they are not charities with people coming to do good. So the US, they have their own international agenda which they are doing which is their right because they have the power now. For the last 100 years they won world wars and won the cold war with the Soviet Union, so they were pursuing their interests. . . . So before the war in Iraq, the US, they have four principles:
>
> - The first one was petrol. It doesn't mean they want the oil or petrol for themselves, but they want to control the trade and movement of oil.
> - The second principle is Israeli security;
> - And after the 90's problems they wanted to lead and fight against Islamic terrorism;
> - And the last principle is to extend the example of American democracy to these parts.
>
> As a soldier and citizen, I understand those principles. I lived in my house in my childhood opposite the American Embassy in Baghdad so I knew the American flag before I even saw the Iraqi flag. I always watched the Marine guards and we had diplomats and Americans as our neighbors and we used to

> play with them as children. We were playing with those teeter tots. My father is an educated person, I come from an educated family. He was influenced by the American message to the world. So I always made a differentiation between American culture and American policy or politics. We don't have a problem with American culture, it's something great that we can be proud of. I was impressed by the American life-style, it's something I admire. But as an educated person I see lots of mistakes in the American policy. (Interview 3/8/2010)

As discussed previously, the imperial image is dynamic and multifaceted. The benevolent imperial image quickly changed to the exploitive imperial image as American behavior started to outrage the Iraqis. Before proceeding to that change and the subsequent behavior change, the actions of the Iraqi sheikhs and other Sunni elites preparing for the arrival of the US forces and their initial overtures to the United States must be discussed.

PREPARING AL ANBAR FOR THE AMERICANS

Sheikh Majed Abd al-Razzaq Ali al-Suleiman, the paramount sheikh of the Dulaym confederation, has provided details on the movements made by the tribes before the Americans invaded Iraq. Sheikh Majed left Iraq for Amman Jordan in the 1990s after a coup attempt made his presence in Iraq precarious, and was in contact with other Iraqi exiles, including Ayad Alawi, Massoud Barzani, and Ahmed Chalabi. It is clear from Sheikh Majed's interviews that he did not like Chalabi (whom he called an "Iranian") or "the Kurds" Barzani and Jalal Talabani (Marine interview, 2009: 124). He recalled meeting with these individuals, particularly Alawi, as well as American intelligence officers in 2001 and 2002 (Marine interview, 2009). The meetings continued in 2003. They discussed on how to enter Iraq from the Saudi border, and devised a plan to use sheep smugglers to gather information on the Iraqi Army's movements in al Anbar. Sheikh Majed stated that he had to dispel American concerns about al Anbar, which included the assumption that it was a bastion of supporters of Saddam Hussein (he blamed Chalabi for that American assumption) (Interview 3/6/2010).

When the war began, Sheikh Majed, several other sheikhs, and several Iraqi military officers were taken to a camp near the Iraqi border where they advised the Iraqi military and civilians not to fight the American/coalition forces (Interview 3/6/2010). When the Americans asked him what he thought about bombing military bases in the province, he said:

> I told them, "Please do not shoot even one bullet in Anbar Province. I can assure you that once you enter Anbar Province, nobody will resist you, neither the tribes nor the military. And I am responsible for what I say. (Marine interview 2009: 126)

The sheikhs had a cause for alarm because in April, 2003, the Americans bombed the Kharbit family farm in Ramadi, Sheikh Majed's old house (Majed, Marine Interview, 2009: 125; Baram, 2005) thinking that Saddam Hussein was hiding there. Twenty-two people were killed, including women, children, and the head of the family, Sheikh Malik Kharbit. The sheikhs were determined to prevent more destruction, and several went to the Americans once they arrived in al Anbar to try to assure them that they would meet no resistance and further bombings were unnecessary. Sheikh Shouka recalled taking a cab to the American position on kilometer 90 of the main road:

> So I talked to the Americans, so I told them all the details. I told them the ex-regime is dismantled. And we the tribes have formed administration councils and police. And we told them when you enter the province nobody will shoot even one bullet at you. And I personally told them I am ready to take two of your girls to show them all of Anbar and bring them back. And they told me we know that Anbar is number one [in supporting Saddam Hussein] and Tikrit number two. I told them it's true that in the war of 1990 the country fell and al Anbar brought back Saddam to power but it's not true that Tikrit is number two and we are number one. So I talked to the American and I explained to him that we don't have that close of a relationship to Saddam Hussein as people think. And the house they have bombed, they have no relation what so ever to politics or anything to do [with Saddam] and that Anbar is ruled by the tribes and they have nothing to do with the ex-regime. So I emphasized if they should go to Anbar no one should fight them there. So they have made another appointment to see me the next day, alone this time, because they were having officials down to see me. I agreed on the next meeting and I said but you should halt on the air strikes. And this is the only promise they made and they fulfilled it to us since then. (Interview 3/17/2010)

Sheikh Hamid Rashid al Alwani was among a group of sheikhs who negotiated with the Americans. He described the experience as follows, with ominous implications for the future interaction between the tribes and the Americans:

> After the American invasion of Iraq in 2003, I was one of the people who went to meet with them outside the al Anbar area, before they entered the city. And we talked with them. There were the army, the intelligence people, and others. We told them advice, if they had taken them, then we would have had less mistakes. One of the things that we told them about [was] not to enter the cities. But they insisted and they went into the cities. At the beginning, at the start of the invasion, we had good coordination with the Americans. And because there was no government at the time, we, the community leaders, took responsibility for the administration. So we had created provincial administration. (Interview, 3/16/2010)

The sheikh's recollections are supported by others'. For example, then-Governor of al Anbar, Mamoun al-Alwani, stated:

> After the fall of the [Saddam Hussein] regime, there was a big vacuum government -wise. The province did not get into a struggle and did not play a role in the fall of the regime. The Coalition forces and the government that was in place here kept the government working normally, so to speak. The tribal leaders were very careful to ensure that they kept the province secure and stable and protected the people. The quiet period lasted until April 2004, maybe even the end of 2004. (Marine interview, 2009: 152)

General Khadim Faris al-Fahadawi also agreed, describing the situation as follows:

> Before the American forces entered the province, the sons of al-Anbar went out to the street and protected the government offices and kept the province secure. The tribes worked together to keep the province settled down, and there was good coordination between the army and other forces and the tribes and the sheikhs.
>
> When the American forces arrived . . . some of the leaders and the sheikhs went out to meet the American forces. There was rumored to be a deal: the sheikhs and the tribes would remain in control of the situation inside the cities, and the American military forces would stay outside of the cities. The sheikhs and the tribes were going to take over administration and security in the cities, and the American forces were going to open an office, which was, maybe, under the name of reconstruction. (Marine interview, 2009: 262)

Kamis al-Alwani, a member of the al Anbar Provincial Council in 2004, described the expectations of the people in al Anbar as follows:

> So the people start to believe, when the Americans come in, they will free us and kill this dictator. And we knew before that the Coalition forces had a good relationship with the neighbors around Iraq, like their relationship with Jordan, Saudi Arabia, and other countries around us. They also thought the same way, when you came inside Kuwait and reconstructed, the same way you were going to do it in Iraq. People believed that's what's going to happen when the Americans come in. (Marine interview 2009: 172)

As this account demonstrates, the tribes were not unhappy with Saddam Hussein's downfall, but they had every intention of retaining control of their geographical area and traditions. Sheikh Majed and the other sheikhs entered Iraq after the American forces entered and immediately appointed Kareem Burjis as governor and Ja'adan Alwani as police chief. Within ten days the government was working, according to Sheikh Majed.

Unfortunately, the relationship with the Americans started to sour quickly. First was the behavior of the American military, which played a key role in the disintegration of positive interactions between the Americans and the sheikhs. Interviewee after interviewee complained that the Americans were ignorant of Iraqi, Arab, and tribal culture, and that the Americans humiliated and mistreated them. Many of our interviewees recited personal experiences that provide insight into the process of humiliation and threat perception that contributed to the disintegration of early stages of cooperation between the Americans and the Sunni tribes. General Ra'ad Hamdani, for example, described an attack on his house where eight people, including four of his children, were present. "'My family was terrified. I had no idea why they were shooting' . . . a soldier pushed him to the ground, handcuffed him, then stood with a boot on his neck" (Rose, 2009: 4). Putting a boot on a person's neck is a grievous insult in tribal culture. Our interview with one sheikh from Fallujah (who requested anonymity) is reflective of this pattern:

> I blame the American forces [for AQI's infiltration into the insurgency and the early support it received]. The American forces, they did not know how to deal with the area and the people of the area. They used excessive unjustified force and also they did not respect the leaders of the people in the area. And this is one of the reasons why the people started to hate the Americans and actually want to fight against them. They were humiliating the tribal leaders in front of the people in the streets, go into houses, destroying furniture, also stealing from the houses, so this made people really hate the Americans. Those are not allegations, those are actions I have witnessed myself and many people have experienced it first hand. . . . Because of all this injustice . . . they started to gather together to want to fight against the Americans. (Interview 3/17/2010)

Many argue that the Americans, unaware of the culture and values of the tribes in al Anbar, overreacted to the Iraqis with violence. Dr. Thamer Ibrahim al-Assafi, a former soldier and, at the time of his interview, a cleric teaching at al Anbar University, recalled:

> Negotiations ensued between the tribes of Anbar and the American forces. . . . An agreement was struck between some of the tribal sheikhs and the American forces for a peaceful entry. After they entered Ramadi, there was a big demonstration, a peaceful demonstration, because they did not approve of an occupier coming into their capital. The American forces did not respect the people who were demonstrating. They dealt with them rather violently. The people's reaction was to pelt the Americans with rocks and tomatoes, and it was a rather negative reaction. They provoked the citizens, that was the first thing that started hatred. (Marine interview, 2009: 33)

Sheikh Majed complained that the Americans heeded to false information and began to arrest innocent people. The Americans "deal with people like they are wrestling" (Interview, 3/6/2010). Major General Tariq al-Thiyabi noted, "In the beginning, when an Iraqi was being searched, he looked upon it as an assault. The way the American forces searched a person, they stopped him, made him turn around, raise his hands, and they searched his body. That sort of posture is insulting for Iraqis. It's even insulting for me to speak about it in front of people" (Marine Interview, 2009: 180). The Americans also took their weapons, which, of course, makes sense from a security standpoint, but it simultaneously threatened social traditions and, ultimately, their ability to protect themselves from AQI. Tribal members are accustomed to being armed; as one interviewee put it, "we are an armed society, basically we are Texas" (Abdullah Khirbit, interviewed 3/22/2010). Sheikh Shouka complained that "the Americans took all the weapons from us, we were defenseless women without any weapons. Even knives we did not have." (Interview 3/17/2010). Sheikh Sabbah's view was particularly harsh: "And the Americans in that area were just murderers. They did not distinguish between normal citizen and terrorist, they just dealt with everyone the same way" (Interview 3/10/2010). Sheikh Shouka also recalled the quick deterioration in the relationship with the Americans:

> So they brought all those opposition leaders, and took them to Sheikh Majed's house from that moment the Americans considered everyone in Anbar as an enemy and they started to do things, bad things. They were humiliating people, crashing into houses with bombs, breaking down the doors, using bombs to open the doors and all that. Eventually this led to natural reaction—resistance. (Interview 3/17/2010)

Generally, this form of humiliation and abuse led to increasing instances of attacks against American forces, and was one powerful motivation for the insurgency that began in al Anbar in the spring of 2003. Violent retaliation against American forces was also a product of tribal culture and values. When innocent people were killed by American forces, vengeance and retaliation was demanded by tribal culture. Tribes that do not seek blood revenge will be looked at as weak, and as having lost honor in the eyes of its members and in the eyes of other tribes in the region.

The second issue that soured relations between the tribes and American forces was de-Ba'athification. The decrees caused many people in al Anbar to lose their jobs, with no prospects for future employment. Men could not support their families. It presented a dual-fold threat to stability in the region—it was humiliating in addition to causing real material hardships. Many of these men had been in the Iraqi Army, had military training, and would become good candidates for the insurgencies that emerged soon after de-Ba'athification's impact was felt. They also received what they considered to be insulting treatment from Bremer when they went to him to object to the de-Ba'athification program. Sheikh Majed said that "the person who was the worst, who did the most damage to American people was Bremer. He was a liar and a thief, snobby, and this made things worse" (Interview 3/6/2010). In his interview with the Marines, Majed said:

> Bremer came over, and the first thing he did was dissolved the Iraqi Army and create an armed enemy against us. This is what we were warning against prior to the liberation. He dissolved all the government institutions and ministries. What he did is just like putting a bomb in this room, and the bomb explodes the whole room. He decimated everything. (2009:127)

Major General John Kelly wrote that the shock and humiliation of having the army dissolved was a strong factor turning the Iraqis in al Anbar against the Americans.

> The army was one of the institutions in Iraq that everyone was proud of—Shi'a and Sunni alike—especially for what it had accomplished in protecting the nation against the Iranians in the 1980s. They perceived the disbanding as international contempt directed toward Iraq as a nation and as a people. They also saw it as the disarming of the nation. In the minds of many, this is when our status as liberators ended and that of occupier began. (Marine Interviews, 2009: *viii*)

As discontent with American policy grew, so did the nationalist resistance. The Sunnis, who had dominated Iraq for decades, now found themselves out of power and unemployed, and many had plentiful arms caches.[1] It seemed to the Sunnis that the Americans were ensuring their marginalization in post-Saddam Iraq. An insurgency was born, and much of it revolved around Sunni identity and the humiliation of that identity. As Hashim writes:

> People fight to gain more . . . resources. It is equally true that people also fight not only to maintain or advance things they value materially, but also for a set of *nonmaterial* values that are subsumed under the rubric of identity. . . . For the Sunni Arabs the downfall of the regime in April 2003 was not only or even primarily the collapse of power and privileges—indeed, many of them had little power and few, if any, privileges—but the entire nationalist edifice that had been in existence for more than eight decades and that had *identified* Iraq with them. (2006: pp. 67–68)

Equally important, the challenge to their identity was synonymous with their loss of power. As one Sunni told Hashim (2006), "We were on top of the system. We had dreams. Now we are the losers. We lost our positions, our status, the security of our families, stability. Curse the Americans. Curse them" (p. 69). Moreover, they were looking at the very real prospect of losing power to the Shi'a community. The CPA's use and promotion of Ahmed Chalabi (a Shi'a) was one sign, as was the American perception, of which they were well aware, the all Sunnis are Ba'athists. Even the suggestion of majority rule was alarming, since the Sunnis are a minority, and three of our interviewees insisted that the Sunnis are not a minority in Iraq (Sheikhs Tariq and Hamid Rashid, and Jalal al Gaood). Some Sunnis have a very negative stereotype of the Shi'a, which only exacerbated their sense of humiliation. Their stereotype depicts the Shi'a as dirty, inferior aliens who secretly act as puppets of Iran and the Persians there. Hashim (2006) quotes one Iraqi Sunni who expresses this stereotype: "They [Shi'a] cannot rule Iraq properly. They cannot take charge of Iraq in the same manner as the Sunni. The Shiites are backwards. They are barbarian savages, they do not know true religion, their's is twisted, it is not the true religion of Muhammad" (pp. 71–72). Given their history with the brutal Iran-Iraq War, and the fact that many Anbaris fought in that war, concerns about the political implications of Shi'a Iraqis' relationship with Shi'a Iran would become increasingly intense as time progressed. In 2004, they were already concerned about Iran and its connection to some of the Iraqis the United States brought into the political scene. Jalal al-Gaood said that, when the Americans invaded:

> They had no plan, unfortunately, and somehow they were run by some, some Iraqi leadership [e.g. Chalabi] that came with the American troops. But certainly we [Sunni sheikhs] felt from the first few months they were Iranian cronies, and it was very clear to us that it was an Iranian scam, and we tried to point that out to the Americans but it was not, they didn't get, the message was not delivered properly. Then I remember very well several times when I sat with the American officers, [I would say] are you guys seriously bringing some religious extremists to control and govern in Iraq? Is this what the Americans look for as a partner in Iraq while you're talking about 9/11, Islamic extremism, Iraq/Iran, AQ. What are you doing? You are just bringing mullahs now, which is the other side of the coin of Islamic extremism, AQ, controlling this country. And somehow this didn't make sense. (Interview 3/8/2010)

The Sunni sheikhs' concerns about Iran increased when Nouri al Maliki was elected prime minister. Although his predecessor, Ayad Allawi, was Shi'a, he was widely regarded as secular and a nationalist. Maliki, on the other hand, had been deeply involved in the Shi'a Dawa party, made illegal under Hussein, and was seen as a secular Shi'a advocate. More will be said in the next chapter on this matter and the challenges it presents.

ONE LAST TRY

Despite the growing insurgency, tribal leaders made one last attempt to work with the United States in the summer of 2004 to negotiate a solution to the growing insurgency in al Anbar. Actually, this effort came along through two initiatives: one from the Marines and the other from the tribal sheikhs. This pattern repeated itself during the Awakening in 2005–2006. The Marines from 1MEF, having stalled out in the first battle for Fallujah under orders from Washington, experimented with the formation of the Fallujah Brigade. They felt, according to Colonel Michael Walker, commander of the 3rd Civil Affairs Group of the Marine force in al Anbar at the time, very frustrated. He called Fallujah a "fiasco . . . probably the single most frustrating experience of my entire career, bar none, nothing even close to being second" (Marine interview 2009: 61). Most importantly, Fallujah threw the Marines off their game plan, to build confidence and trust in the Iraqi population. Now, they had to "start thinking outside the box because we've got a mess on our hands" (p. 62). The Marines began talking with Liaison Officers (LNO) in Kuwait and Jordan to explore the idea of having Arabs from other countries help with the economy in al Anbar. In the process, they made the connection between increasing stability in al Anbar as a necessary prerequisite to economic investment and growth.

Colonel Walker was introduced by Colonel Dave Harlan, the LNO in Jordan, to Talal al-Gaood, a successful businessman and son of the sheikh of the Albu Nimr tribe in the Dulaym Confederation (and brother of our interviewee Jajal al Gaood). Al-Gaood had come to the same conclusion about the need for a coordinated effort by the tribal leaders and the Marines to stabilize al Anbar. Talal al-Gaood had started working on this issue in December, 2003, and interacted with a businessman from Texas, Ken Wischkaemper, an expert in agriculture.

After making contact with Colonel Michael Walker, Talal al-Gaood organized a business conference in Bahrain, and then moved to enlist Wischkaemper's and others' help in organizing another conference in Amman in July, 2004. Wischkaemper had warned al-Gaood that they would have to be careful of certain camps in Washington, D.C. who were fundamentally against negotiating with the Sunnis. In a memo quoted by Perry (2010) before the conference (May 8), he wrote:

> Please know that there is a deep, deep, divide at the Pentagon. It is the Z group [the Zell group—Wolfowitz, Feith, and their allies] versus the Rum [R] group. Please know that the R group favors our methodology at the expense of the methodology of the Z group. . . . It appears that the R group may be finally gaining the upper hand. Please know that your and your guys' support is of extreme importance. (pp. 26–27)

The conference was scheduled for July 18–20, 2004. In attendance on the American side were Wischkaemper; Jerry Jones, a special assistant to Defense Secretary Rumsfeld; Ambassador Evan Galbraith; James Clad, a counselor for the Overseas Private Investment Corporation; Lieutenant Colonel Harlan; Major Pat Maloy; and others. The topic was supposed to be economic development in Iraq. There were 78 Iraqis in attendance (Perry 2010).

Al-Gaood and the Iraqis, however, had a much larger agenda. Along with businessmen, there were representatives of the insurgency. Colonel Walker believed they were very well organized, and had security, economy, and governance organizations (Walker, Marine interview 2009: 66). He believed that 23 of the 78 Iraqis in the conference had strong ties to the national Iraqi insurgencies (Perry, 2010: 43). There was also one person present who represented 16 very important insurgent groups, known as "the Messenger," otherwise known as "Dr. Ismail" (Rose, 2009; Perry, 2010). Walker later told General Conway that he believed that the Messenger represented the military arm of the insurgency, while the others represented the political arm (Rose, 2009).

Al-Gaood held a small meeting with Dr. Ismail and several Americans, Jones, Clad, Walker, and Harlan. Dr. Ismail gave them a list of demands on the second day of the conference:

> It began with three "non-negotiable points"—that Iraq "should be viewed as one united country"; that the occupation must end, "even if that has to happen in stages"; and that "the wealth of Iraq should be used for the benefit of Iraqis and should not be siphoned off by others." To this was added a significant rider: "We don't mind participation by American companies. As a matter of fact, we encourage their participation."
>
> The document continued with eight "urgent immediate demands." These were: the establishment of a new Iraqi Army; the disbanding of sectarian militias; the withdrawal of U.S. forces from the cities; the release of political prisoners; an end to interference in Iraqi affairs by neighboring countries; pressure on the Kurds to "cease the rhetoric of separation from Iraq"; a promise that the U.S. would stop describing insurgents as "terrorists"; and, finally, a pledge to "continue political dialogue between Iraqis and Americans. (Rose, 2009: 2)

Walker asked for evidence that the insurgents were sincere and that Dr. Ismail spoke for them. He asked for a cease-fire as a test of their credibility and intentions. The cease-fire never occurred.

In addition to the insurgent representatives, General Ra'ad Hamdani was invited to the conference. He came with a plan in mind. First, he told the Americans that it was "wrong and dangerous to disband the army . . . that there would be chaos, and external forces interested" (Interview 3/8/2010). He suggested the creation of a replacement force for the army, a local force (Interview, 3/8/2010). At a second conference in August, Hamdani provided a more detailed plan for the creation of an Auxiliary Security Force with an initial 5,000 soldiers and 100 commanders (Perry, 2010; Interview with Hamdani 3/ 8 /2010). The force would not be a local militia, but responsible to the American forces and the Iraqi Ministry of Defense. Hamdani believed that this would separate the national resistance from foreign forces (i.e., AQI). He argued that reversing the de-Ba'athification process and resurrecting the Iraqi Army would be necessary, because the resistance was from the former army (Perry, 2010). Colonel John Coleman, General Conway's chief of staff, attended the August meeting. General Conway approved of the proposal, and Colonel Coleman took the proposal to Washington where it was immediately killed. Hamdani has expected it to be approved within 72 hours and was shocked when it was rejected (Interview 3/8/2010). On his return trip to Baghdad via Amman, Coleman discovered he had been declared *persona non grata* by the US Embassy, and not permitted to enter the country other than for a brief overnight stay. Perry (2010) provides solid evidence that the proposal's death sentence was a product of State Department's anger over perceived Marine involvement in diplomacy and pressure from Allawi, who was angry about the negotiations and talks in Jordan.

Two journalists who have done extensive research on these events, David Rose and Mark Perry, argue that Pentagon documents show that Donald Rumsfeld at one point found this idea intriguing. He told Bremer and the military commanders in Iraq to "'elicit help from the Sunni tribal leaders'" (Rose, 2009: 3) and asked Deputy Secretary of State Armitage for support. Armitage opposed the idea, calling it a "colossal mistake (Rose, 2009:3) and General George Casey, commander in Iraq, advocated a more kinetic approach to the insurgency (Rose, 2009). General Conway, on the other hand, supported it strongly:

> The Marine Corps backed the proposals from the top. In an e-mail written on August 30, after Walker and Coleman had met al-Hamdani, Lieutenant General Conway wrote that he "had advised our higher headquarters as to the contacts and [was] encouraged to continue the dialogue. Our objective remains to reduce attacks and get at the essence of the insurgency in Al Anbar. I consider the discussions a non-kinetic approach to a military objective and believe we should pursue that option. . . . We consider the effort one of the more successful engagement programs that we have and are looking to 'operationalize' the effort as we work to reduce the intimidation and murder campaign." Conway also noted that he did not believe "the discussions rise to the level of political issues or run counter to P[rime] M[inisterial] or ambassadorial objectives." (Rose, 2009: 3)

This opportunity was crushed by opponents in both Iraq and Washington. The Iraqi interim prime minister, Ayad Allawi, did not like the idea of any kind of independent military unit in al Anbar. Wolfowitz continued his approach to oppose negotiating with the Sunnis. At the same time, the State Department became very territorial, complaining of "rogue" Defense Department personnel engaging in diplomacy, which was their bailiwick (Rose, 2009).

THE INSURGENCY

The insurgency in Iraq began in the summer of 2003. The first bombing in AQI's opening salvo took place in August when the Jordanian embassy and UN headquarters in Baghdad were attacked. There is some debate as to whether or not Saddam Hussein's regime planned for a postwar insurgency, assuming that they would not be able to withstand American firepower. Hashim (2006) argues that it is most likely that the regime did prepare for a postwar insurgency, but that it was expected to be limited to Ba'athist supporters rather than a general uprising by the population. But the insurgency was much more complex, and much less well organized, than an insurgency led by former Ba'athists would be. As Packer put it, the "Iraqi insurgency had no Mao, no Ho, no clear and popular political agenda" (2005: 302).

The insurgencies varied in structure from those that were hierarchical and followed a chain of command, to those that were small cells. In between were the horizontally organized groups based upon tribe, clan, or kinship relations (Beehner, 2005; Hashim, 2006). Among the more organized hierarchical organizations operating in al Anbar was the Islamic Army in Iraq, which was formed in 2002, and declared its existence in May 2003. Its members were Iraqi nationals, including former military members, but they were not strong Ba'athists or interested in returning to the former regime. Their goal was to expel the United States from Iraq (Cordesman, 2007). The Mujahideen Army of Iraq started its activities in 2004. It was also national Iraqi in composition with some Saddam-era officers, but Salaafist in orientation. The central goal was an Islamic government with adherence to Sharia law. It may also have been an umbrella organization including other groups (Cordesman, 2007; Hashim, 2006). Another group, the Ansar al Sunnah Army, grew out of the terrorist organization, Ansar al-Islam in September, 2003. Its goal was also an Islamic state in Iraq. The Iraqi Resistance Movement—1920 Revolutionary Brigade was formed in June 2003, composed of former army officers. It was larger; an umbrella organization of several different brigades with the goal of establishing a nationalist government after driving the United States out (Cordesman, 2007). The Snake's Head Movement was a Ba'athist organization with associations with some of the tribes of al Anbar (Hashim, 2006; for a more complete list of insurgent groups in Iraq as a whole see Hashim, 2006). The initial response of American forces was to focus on the former regime leaders, and they succeeded in killing Saddam Hussein's sons Husay and Qusay, and capturing Saddam Hussein. However, this did not stop the insurgency. The supporters of the former regime splintered, but the numbers of insurgents actually increased in response to the aggression and force used by the Americans (Montgomery, 2009).

With the fluid borders, non-Iraqis could and did enter Iraq to join the insurgencies. Among them was Jordanian-born Abu Musab al-Zarqawi. He was a Jordanian with a lengthy career running afoul of authority, beginning with an arrest for drug possession and sexual assault in the mid-1980s (Kirdar, 2011). He was exposed to radical Islam while in prison, and went to Afghanistan in 1989 to fight in the jihad against the Soviets (but they were already leaving). However, he was exposed to al Qaeda there, and became more radical in his beliefs. He met his future mentor, Sheikh Abu Muhammadal-Maqdisi, in Peshawar. After returning with Maqdisi to Jordan in 1992, he formed the extremist group Baya'at al-Imam. Zarqawi was arrested again in 1993 for the possession of weapons and explosives and sentenced to fifteen years, but was released under a general amnesty in 1999. While in prison, Zarqawi and Maqdisi were able to expand the influence of Baya'at al Imam and came to Osama bin Laden's attention (Kirdar, 2011). Upon his release he went to Afghanistan again, setting up a training camp for radical Muslims. After the 9/11 attack, Zarqawi and his fighters went into Iran, and then moved between Iran, Kurdish Iraq, Syria, and Lebanon before returning to Jordan in 2002 (Kirdar, 2011; Hashim, 2006). During this time, the group acquired a new name, Jama'at al-Tawhid wa al-Jihad (TwJ).

Seif al-Adel, AQ's security director, met with Zarqawi and helped Zarqawi's people move into Iraq before the American invasion.[2] According to Kirdar (2011) Adel:

> Further funneled an inflow of Arab Islamists through Syria into Iraq where Zarqawi had joined a number of Arab Islamists already based in the territory controlled by the Kurdish Islamist group Ansar al-Islam. While in Iraq, Zarqawi traveled frequently to the "Sunni Triangle"—a 100–square-mile area between Baghdad, Ramadi, and Tikrit—deepening his network, recruiting fighters, and establishing bases. Zarqawi's expansion of his weapons and fighter smuggling networks made him the default conduit for most, if not all, foreign fighters—including members of TwJ and other Islamist terrorist groups—flowing into Iraq in anticipation of the U.S.-led invasion. He became the default "emir" of Islamist terrorists in Iraq. (p. 3)

In October, 2004, Zarqawi pledged allegiance to Osama bin Laden and was in turn recognized as the leader of al Qaeda in Iraq (AQI) (Montgomery, 2009; Hashim, 2006). This recognition did not come easily. Al Qaeda central, specifically Ayman al Zawahiri, was concerned with the brutality and lack of strategic thinking in Zarqawi's behavior. They also worried about the targeting of the Shi'a by Zarqawi's organization (Whiteside, 2014). In fact, by this time, Zarqawi's TwJ had increased its attacks on Shi'a targets, provoking deeper and deeper sectarian hostility.[3]

In his interview, former General Ra'ad Hamdani provided his impression of when and how fighters who eventually joined AQI entered Iraq:

> When [insurgents] came to Iraq they came step by step. They did not come all at once. Before Feb 2003 there was nothing called al Qaida in Iraq. But when the war was imminent in Iraq, there was a call for jihad to fight against Americans because of the war. Although AQ hated Saddam all the time, and his party, because they were considered anti-Muslims or secular but when the war was imminent they have changed their minds—the enemy of my enemy is my friend. At that time in the unit in the army which I was leading, we had special forces training school. And we had Arab forces coming to that school. I was busy because my appointment was in the south of Iraq so I was busy how to block the invasion but I had an urgent message from the Dean of the academy that I have to be present. I had a call from the responsible people at the school, and they said we have a problem with these people, we are not used to this kind of people because we usually train military organized people but these people have some kind of weird behavior. So he told me you can go and see for yourself. So I went to see a group of them. When I talked to them I discovered these people were not working any defensive plan we would have, because they have their own ideas, their own agenda. And you would feel lots of suspicion for such groups. So I phoned Saddam Hussein and I said can I apologize for not accepting those people for training because we are busy making plans for the invasion, making the defenses. He agreed and they were transferred to other places. So we got the busses and transported them. This was the beginning. During the war I heard these people were fighting in Baghdad and they had the reputation of being good fighters. After the invasion the Iraqi borders were open so any people could come and cross the border. (Interview, 3/8/2010)

Ultimately, the leadership of AQI was non-Iraqis, while the vast majority of the foot soldiers were Iraqis. In the beginning there was tribal support for the insurgency, including AQI, although it was not uniform (R. Hamdani interview, 3/8/2010).

AQI received initial support from the Anbaris for various reasons. First, they brought money and, as Sheikh Majed explained:

> The reason why people started to join AQ was because there were lots of unemployed people, thousands of people were in the Army and they just dissolved it, also all the officials from the Ba'ath party were also kicked out so of course the person who would come paying money, you would want to eat to live. So the Americans created all that, I wonder until now if that was intended or stupidity, I don't understand it, in my opinion the Americans are smart but I don't understand how they would allow this to happen. (interview 3/6/2010)

At the same time, AQI held the "liberation narrative" (General John Allen, Interview 2/9/2010). Ra'ad Hamdani described their infiltration process as follows:

> In the Iraqi culture and Arab culture the tribes would welcome any foreigner for three days and three nights without asking them any questions. They were coming to the guest houses and staying there and they were increasing in numbers. Because the numbers were so large the guest houses were not enough so they were put in their houses as well. Even to the point that the homes were not enough and they put them in the mosque. They started influencing the people through religious and emotional ways. People saw these people coming without any belongings. They had only their machine gun or weapon, coming to fight for Iraq, and the people were impressed and felt good or nice about such people. And they were such a large force they were leading themselves, and they had their own training camps. They organized training camps for themselves. (Interview 3/8/2010)

EXPLANATIONS AND SUMMARY

We conclude this chapter with a discussion of the analytical factors presented in the last chapter: social identity and images.

Threats to Sunni Tribal Identity by the United States

The Sunni tribal interviewees from al Anbar perceived both threat and opportunity in the US invasion, consistent with the exploitation/opportunity characteristics of the imperial image they held of the United States. They saw little distinction between themselves and Iraq. Their tribal Sunni identity overlapped largely with their identity as Iraqis. They believed that they personify Iraq (Sheikh Majed interview, 3/6/2010; A. Khirbit interview, 3/22/2010). After Saddam's overthrow, the tribes had three central concerns. First, they wanted to maintain their control over power and resources. This involved resisting equal representation (since Sunnis are the minority) and competition with other tribes. Second, they wanted "stability within the tribal power structure" (Todd, 2006: Ch. 4, p. 2). In other words, they wanted to retain the traditional balance between individual achievement and advancement within the tribe, and the tribal hierarchy of power. Shortly after the overthrow of Saddam Hussein, many of the true sheikhs who had gone into hiding for protection from Saddam reemerged (Allen Interview 2/9/2010). Third, each tribe wanted a position for itself in the post-Saddam political environment (Todd, 2006). Given the Sunnis' historical role in Iraqi governance, and their view of themselves as the personification of Iraq, they expected the United States to select them to lead the post–Saddam Hussein Iraq. Not only did the United States fail to meet these expectations but the US policies in post-invasion and occupation Iraq humiliated the Sunnis in a variety of ways through their treatment at the hands of the US military and its disjointed and aggressive response to insecurity in the region. Both of these constitute a very serious violation of tribal values that heightened the importance, or salience, of tribal identity. These events also greatly increased their sense of threat from what they once viewed as an imperialist actor. In this process, the emphasis on opportunity presented by the imperialist shifted toward a perception of threat.

The Sunni tribes lost resources, power, and status under the de-Ba'athification program. As mentioned above, many Anbari men served in the Iraqi Army, which was never seen as Saddam Hussein's army, but was a symbol of national pride. When they were summarily dismissed in 2003 they lost their sources of income, and could not feed their families. Thus, their role as providers for their immediate families, and in the case of tribal sheikhs, for larger dimensions of dependents, was destroyed. As Jalal al Gaood noted:

> What happened and how we can bring together both the tribal structure in piece with this new situation, because in all honesty what happened, looked at from a Sunni perspective, looked like a revolution against us. The target was the Sunni community. (Interview 3/8/2010)

In social identity terms, the social comparison of the Sunni tribes of al Anbar went from being very positive to negative, with no way to reverse the change of fortune. Overtures made to the Americans for cooperation in preventing civil war were dismissed. The Sunnis were faced with the prospect of losing power to the numerical majority Shi'a, which was not just a challenge to their self-image, but a perceived grave threat to their very survival. Many al Anbar Sunnis fought in the Iran-Iraq War and had firsthand experience with brutal warfare with Iran. The Sunnis we interviewed expressed universal fear of Iran, and they were ambivalent about the loyalties of Iraq's Shi'a population. They did believe, however, that the al Maliki government was an Iranian agent. Their evolving perceptions of AQI and Iran will be discussed in the next chapter in greater detail.

Adding to this the perception that they, the Iraqi Sunnis, were the definition of Iraq as a nation, it is not surprising that the al Anbar tribes gave some measure of support to the national insurgents and AQI. They lost their power and prestige, and they feared they would lose their country and nation to the Shi'a—and through them—to Iran. Moreover, the Americans believed they were all supporters of the previous regime, and would not listen to their overtures for cooperation, thus tilting tribal perception of the US imperialist to one of exploitative threat rather than opportunity.

Tribal Image of the United States

Our analysis of our interviews and those done by the Marines leads to the assessment that initially, as the invasion began, the tribal leaders appeared to perceive the United States through the imperial image in its benevolent form. They promised a nonviolent entrance into Anbar and expected to be called upon to help shape the new Iraq. When their overtures were rejected, they saw the United States through the imperialist image in its harmful, exploitive form. As discussed in the previous chapter, the strategy typically used in response to perceived imperial powers is to submit, because resistance is futile. However, in this case, it is arguable that the imperial image of the United States began to weaken, at least in terms of the capability dimension. The nationalist insurgency picked up steam after Fallujah 1, and Anbar became an extremely violent place, where coalition forces experienced high numbers of casualties. This made the overwhelming power of the coalition questionable, and hence encouraged the national resistance. In addition, the insurgents regarded Fallujah 1 as a victory. They believed that they had won; they had defeated the Marines, and did not understand that the Marines were forced to stop fighting because of political pressure (Walker, Marine interview, 2009). These developments caused a diminution in the perception of the superior capability of the imperialist, and changed their assessment of the strategies available to them.

Sunni Tribal Image of al Qaeda 2003–2004

The data collected during our interviews and from those done by the Marines indicate that the image of AQI was that of an ally in 2004.

The Ally Image: None of the interviewees admitted to having thought positively of AQI, but they do report that others in Anbar did so, and that they regarded AQI as an ally against the Americans. The best description and explanation of the early acceptance of AQI came from our interview with General Ra'ad Hamdani as follows (quoted at length above):

> They (AQI) started influencing the people through religious and emotional ways. People saw these people coming without any belongings. They had only their machine gun or weapon, coming to fight for Iraq, and the people were impressed and felt good or nice about such people. . . . So people were impressed by them. (Interview 3/8/2010)

Abdullah Khirbit, son of a sheikh, described AQI's influence as follows:

> You see there is a problem with AQ because they [represent themselves as] the honest people, they are the legitimate people, they represent God, according to their theory which they very well established. There was a time when

> just talking about them would lead to you would get attacked by civilians, you would get attacked by people just because how dare you talk about AQ because they are fighting the Americans. They made a very good effort in making the picture of the Americans look bad actually, anybody with common sense would see their tricks, but you know public doesn't have common sense. (Interview 3/22/2010)

The foreigners were seen as Arab allies coming to fight for the people in Anbar and to liberate them from the Americans who they increasingly no longer saw as a benevolent imperial but an exploitative presence threatening to their tribal identity and, by extension, to Iraq itself. They also seemed, at first, to have the interests of the Anbari people in mind, because they brought money, whereas the de-Ba'athification program brought poverty. Here we can see the intersection of material and identity-based motives.

American Images of the Sunni Tribes

The Rogue Image: The image through which Saddam Hussein was perceived was the rogue image and it was easily transferred to the Sunnis in al Anbar, who were assumed to be strong supporters of his regime by policy makers in the Bush administration. The rogue image is the image of a bad seed, an inferior actor in terms of culture and capability, and harmful in intentions. The normal policy inclination when confronted with a rogue is to crush when possible. The image was not universally shared. Indeed, Wischkamer warned Talal al Gaood of a very deep divide in the Pentagon about the Sunnis (Perry, 2010). The camp associated with Paul Wolfowitz was very hostile toward and contemptuous of the Sunnis of Anbar. Wolfowitz referred to them as "Nazis," which is a strong indication of cultural contempt for them (Perry, 2010). The assumption that the United States, with some allies, could go into Iraq with a relatively small force and quickly depose the dictatorship is a reflection of the civilian policy planners' perception of their inferiority in capability.

Even some of the Americans involved in the 2004 negotiations sparked by Talal al Gaood appear to have this image. Mike Walker, for example, recalls that he wanted to break the ice, so he walked over to a group of Iraqis before the day's conference began and said "I told them that I understood a lot of their complaints. . . . But I told them that they could stop their cheerleading about Saddam. I was pretty blunt: 'He was corrupt, a complete dictator, he stole money and food from his own people.' I didn't raise my voice, I didn't get angry, but I told them 'The Ba'ath Party is as dead as the Nazi Party'. And, I told them to stop defending Saddam because he was a monster and they knew it. They got the point' (quoted in Perry, 2010: 41–42). This account puts the rogue image in stark relief. Recall the preferred strategy of dealing with a rogue actor is to crush, punish, and discipline in order to induce obedience. This sounds more like a lecture to naughty children than an ice-breaker at a conference with major stakeholders in a war-torn society.

A number of the tactical decisions made during the early years of the war also reflect the rogue image. The disrespectful treatment of the Anbaris, the disregard of tribal culture, the dismissal of their grievances regarding their treatment and inability to protect themselves, and the orders for Fallujah 1 are all attributable to the rogue image. A consequence of holding this perception is that the perceived culture does not deserve attention, and agreements or terms can be changed or dictated. As a consequence, the city of Fallujah, which the United States had agreed not to enter, was attacked in punishment for the murders of four Blackwater contractors and the desecration of their bodies. Again, it is important to emphasize that the rogue image was prevailing among policy makers, though there were many who did not have the image. General Conway, for example, when ordered to embark on Fallujah 1 was reportedly furious, believing that "sending his marines into Fallujah to look for murderers would only turn the people of the city against him. Civilians would be caught in the crossfire" (Perry, 2010: 16).

CONCLUSION

This chapter concludes with details of the events in 2004. By this time, the insurgency is in full swing, al Qeada has received a statement of loyalty from Zarqawi's Jama'at al-Tawhid wa al-Jihad becoming AQI, and gained adherents. The Sunni tribes tried and failed to work with the Americans to prevent an insurgency from breaking out, and to stop it once it developed. They lost virtually everything: their power, their prestige, their jobs, and, in their minds, their country. The Americans were also deeply frustrated. Those with the rogue image of the Sunnis provoked them through policies like de-Ba'athification, and they did not expect and did not recognize the budding insurgency. Nor did they understand why Iraq had not followed the course of action they expected of their perceived rogue actor. Meanwhile, many military officers understood what the failure to develop a Phase IV plan was beginning to cost them, and they scrambled to try to change certain tactics that only further fueled the insurgency.

We argue throughout this chapter that social identity and images play a central, although not the only, role in these developments. In the next chapter we examine important changes in perceptions and images that unfolded in al Anbar, which led to a change in the behavior of the Americans and the tribes. These changes also include shifts in the Sunni tribes' perceptions of AQI and, together, shifts of perceptions by the Americans and the tribes, which begin to lay groundwork for increased cooperation and stability in the al Anbar region.

NOTES

1. Whiteside (2014) points out that the "Iraqi Army depots were left unguarded for months after the invasion and further abandoned after the disastrous disbanding decision. Opportunists reburied these elsewhere and sold them to insurgent groups for years afterward" (personal correspondence).

2. Adel was a merely an advocate for al Qaeda's support for Zarqawi. He encouraged bin Laden to give Zarqawi funding for a training camp in Pakistan after the latter's 1999 release from prison (Kirdar, 2011).

3. Concerns about Zarqawi's violent tactics increased in January 2006 to the point that AQI and five affiliated groups for the Mujahideen Shura Council, which was led by the member groups' leaders, but Zarqawi was not included. His influence appears to have diminished, but one contrary interpretation is that he was purposely leaving the limelight in order to reduce the perception that foreign fighters dominated AQI (Whiteside, personal correspondence, 2015). Zarqawi was killed in June 2006.

Chapter 4

The Violence Escalates

By late 2004 al Anbar was wracked with violence. The insurgency that the United States did not anticipate, and was unprepared for, accelerated and al Anbar became the most dangerous place in Iraq. Meanwhile, Secretary of Defense Rumsfeld denied that there was an insurgency in Iraq and forbade the use of the word (Ferguson, 2008: 316). In 2004 the insurgency was still multidimensional, a mixture of national resistance groups and al Qaeda. It continued to be fueled by worsening economic circumstances, resentment of the American occupation, and decreasing personal security (Ferguson, 2008: 318). The government in the province was weakened after the kidnapping of Governor Burgis's sons and his subsequent resignation. The police also collapsed, as the chief of police in Ramadi began to cooperate with insurgents, and police officers' lives were threatened by the insurgents (West, 2005).

There is no statistical evidence of tribal support for the insurgencies in al Anbar, whether it be nationalist insurgencies or al Qaeda. Interviewees, many of whom may have supported the insurgencies at one point, describe general support among the populace of al Anbar in 2004. Influenced by imams, people "started to support the mujahideen with ammunition and weapons, housing and accommodations—everything" (Marine interview General Nuri al-Fahadawi, 2009: 196). Another General, Haqi Ali Hameed, explained their support as follows:

> Some [insurgents] were religious groups, and others were nationalist groups, and some were military groups. Some of them were from the previous army, and some of them were from the previous security forces. Some groups were Ba'ath party members and people who were close to the previous regime. At that time, we thought that they had the right and the privilege to fight back and to protect themselves. So that's why they received wide support from the Iraqi people, especially in the middle area, like Baghdad, Diyala, Salah ad Din, and at the

> top of the list, al Anbar. . . . These groups started by attacking the occupation forces. They depended on light weapons. They were funded by people who believed in their cause or maybe they donated their own money. (Marine interview, 2009: 223–224)

Al Qaeda, on the other hand, was better armed and funded. They enticed support through the money they could provide, and by capturing the "liberation narrative" (General Allen interview 2/9/2010). Tribal support for al Qaeda was varied. It was not a situation in which entire tribes supported al Qaeda, but rather factions of tribes offered their support. As General Hamdani explained, "you don't have whole tribes joining al Qaeda or fighting against al Qaeda, it's always divided . . . a part of the tribe will be with al Qaeda, another part will be against. It depends on their personal history with al Qaeda from the start. If they have problems with them they will be against them. If they had not been terrorized they would be with them" (interview 3/8/2010). All of the tribes were targeted by al Qaeda, but some suffered more than others. The smaller, weaker, and poorer tribes suffered the most. Larger tribes had more resources and were better able to form militias to resist al Qaeda (General Allen interview 2/9/2010).

As Hamdani implies above, al Qaeda came into Iraq posing as liberators, but quickly revealed their true tactics and strategy, and began to terrorize the local population. They implemented a systematic plan to eliminate potential power competitors. Sheikhs, former soldiers, police officers, government officials, doctors, professors, and anyone thought to associate with the Americans were assassinated. As Major General Tariq al Thiyabi put it, "If we had an American convoy roll down the street, and one of the people happened to wave to them, that person could consider himself dead" (Marine interview, 2009: 181). Over time, they also began to target the other insurgent groups. Al Qaeda gave members of other insurgent groups the stark choice of joining al Qaeda, or death (Marine interview with General al Fahada; Sheikh Aakab al Gaood interview 3/15/2010; Khirbit interview 3/22/2010). In a report issued on August 17, 2006, 1MEF determined that beginning in December, 2005, al Qaeda began its program to eliminate, subsume, marginalize, or co-opt the nationalist insurgents. This effort began "shortly after the national elections in December 2005, when nationalist insurgent groups cooperated to prevent AQI from disrupting polling throughout al-Anbar. Faced with this blatant challenge to their hegemony, AQI destroyed . . . the sole rival nexus of insurgent leadership in al-Anbar" (2006: 2).

General Hamdani described the efforts of AQI to destroy the tribal system, starting with the sheikhs:

> [The people who were most negatively] influenced . . . by the influence of those strangers who came and settled was (sic) the tribal leaders. Because what was

> happening is they would be talking to someone of no importance and they would support their ideas and they would tell them, why you don't go now and replace the sheikh? Replace the tribal leaders and you become the new tribe leader. So the first struggles started between AQ and tribal leaders because of personal power and personal gain, not because of national interest and being interested in Iraq. They used terrorist means to keep things under their control unless they were faced by let's say a strong tribal leader who would use force to drive them back. Otherwise they just had supreme command, they would use terror and rape and whatever to keep people under their control. On that tribal level the people are simple, they don't have any big political awareness and they don't understand what's going on. They are just influenced by emotions and actions that're happening around them. So if there is something good they are happy, if there is something bad they are sad. This is the answer to your question. It did not start because of national interest; it was started because of personal fights over authority between the tribal leader and the new stranger who is coming to challenge his power. (Interview 3/8/2010)

Al Qaeda divided al Anbar into sectors, and each sector had an al Qaeda cell headed by an "emir." The emirs were foreigners, and were under the direction of Abu Musab al Zarqawi, the Jordanian national. The emirs had tremendous power, the power to "kill, to steal, to do anything he liked" (Marine interview with Major General Khadim al Dukaymi, 2009: 263). The foot soldiers were Iraqis, and they are universally described by our interviewees as criminals, lowlifes, gullible boys, and those from bad families. Sheikh Sabah stated that al Qaeda "brainwashed" young men (Marine interview, 2009: 145).The terror used to make the people submit to al Qaeda authority was grotesque, including killing people in front of their families, beheading them, using torture, hiding bodies in the desert so they could not be buried, and imposing a variety of rules. Men had to grow their beards, women could not go out in public without a male relative escort, women could not go to school, smoking and music were forbidden, and tomatoes and cucumbers could not be placed in the same plastic bags (Aakab al Gaood interview 3/15/2010). Sheikh Sabah told one graphic story that illustrates al Qaeda's brutality:

> When you went from al Qaim to Ramadi, which is 300 kilometers, you would find tens of bodies without heads alongside the road. Those were marks of people murdered by AQ. Most of them would be innocent people. . . . The year 2005 when AQ controlled al Qaim area, they killed four people from the Salmani tribe. And they left the bodies in the street. This is in July 2005. And they forbid anyone to bury them. In Iraq it is very hot that time of year so the bodies started to decompose. The smell was terrible. Ten days later they said ok, it's allowed if you want to bury them, but they left IEDs inside the bodies. When their families went to get the bodies to bury them, they detonated the bomb. They killed another 8 of the families of those people. This is just a small example of how AQ terrorized the people. They were murderers and criminals.

> Islam religion is not like this. Islam is a religion of compassion. In Islam you don't go killing people without reason like that. They indiscriminately were just killing anyone. (interview 3/10/2010)

Al Qaeda's force became increasingly criminalized, particularly as more Iraqis joined. They drew upon criminal networks who had no political agenda, but who used AQI tactics to rob and abuse people. Al Qaeda also destroyed the infrastructure of al Anbar. They blew up people, bridges, schools, government buildings, hospitals, factories, cell phone towers, and anything else that could keep al Anbar functioning (Marine interview with Staff Brigadier General Haqi Ali Hameed; Deane, 2010). Sheikh Ahmed Albu Risha recalled:

> They killed a lot of personnel from the police. They destroyed the Iraqi Army. They destroyed the infrastructure of the country. They attacked schools. They attacked university professors. They forbade involvement in any political dialogue. The situation became unbearable. The sheikhs and the brains left the province—professors, teachers, and doctors—they all went to Jordan and Syria. Al-Qaeda roved the country. We set up security forces around our compounds, and we stayed here. . . . Infrastructure services were really bad. Education and health care were bad. Al-Qaeda took over the Ramadi hospital, the Department of Education, the university, the oil infrastructure, and they were the rulers. (Marine interview, 2009: 46)

Experiencing this brutality affected tribal identities. They became stronger, as people retreated into the group that could best provide safety (Jalal al Gaood interview 3/8/2010). Many of the sheikhs left the country, often at the request of their tribes, to avoid being killed. This would later cause complications because lower-level sheikhs were left in al Anbar to make decisions that would normally be made by the paramount sheikh. At this time, the tribal leaders made a key realization that fundamentally changed the dynamic in the province. The tribal leaders began to realize that al Qaeda's goal was not the liberation of Iraq, but the elimination of the tribal system itself.

The experience with AQI's violence gradually eroded the ally image of AQI. It was replaced with the barbarian image, as is illustrated in the following quote:

> As time went by they started to treat their hosts badly because they were now the force, they had the power. . . . Then, later on, they started to influence and tried to put pressure on the tribes to follow their own laws and rules that they have set. (Ra'ad Hamdani, Interview 3/8/2010)

Many interviewees expressed the loss of power experienced by the Anbar tribesmen such as Aakab al Gaood's description as follows:

> One of the things that AQ used for their benefit was the policy of the American Army in Iraq. They [the Americans] did not allow citizens to carry weapons in their houses. Because Anbar area is a tribal community, it means every house should have at least one of these weapons. The people were afraid to keep the weapons at home, otherwise they would go to jail. So they started hiding or giving away those weapons. At the same time, the AQ militias have advanced weapons and lots of them, so they had the upper hand. The normal citizens did not have any power to fight against AQ. (Interview 3/15.2010)

Sheikh Shouka confirms this experience by also expressing the power imbalance relative to AQI, and the confusing behavior of the imperialists:

> The Americans took all the weapons from us, we were defenseless women without any weapons. Even knives we did not have. Why AQ had all kinds of weapons and they could go and come as they pleased, and the Americans came and gave me a gift of a pistol and then the next day they came and searched my house and took it. (Interview 3/17/2010)

Many interviewees described what they perceived as the inferior cultural values of AQI. They began to see AQI commit numerous atrocities and violate basic cultural and religious beliefs and thus deem them as below the cultural standing and sophistication of their own group:

> Al Qaeda was acting like religious authorities making things right and wrong as they wish not according to Islamic Sharia law, and it was all, all this was coming from Iran just to destroy the Sunni, Sunni and Islamism. . . . People were terrorized by those acts, and they were stealing the (unintelligible) of our people so they were really criminals, stealing, raping, killing, murderers, so people saw the real face of them. And from the beginning we heard they were against Islam and we saw that it was true. (Sheikh Majed, Interview 3/6/2010)

These statements are a reflection of the barbarian image: superior in power, inferior in culture, and harmful in intentions. While the people in al Anbar and the tribal leaders in particular were faced with rising AQI terrorism in their home province, they were also experiencing a compounding threat to their identity. At the same time they were experiencing AQI's brutality, the Anbaris felt abandoned by a Shi'a-dominated government in Baghdad that, in their perception, was increasingly controlled by Iran. The government failed to pay Iraqi Security Forces in al Anbar, it also undermined and attacked Sunni political leaders, and gave little support to local government and institutions in al Anbar (1MEF, 2006: 1). Attacks against Sunnis in Baghdad by Shi'a militias continued unabated. When elections were held in January 2005 to elect a transitional government, the Sunnis boycotted, believing that legitimate elections were not possible while the country was occupied

(Hashim, 2006: 76).[1] In al Anbar, the result of this boycott was the election of members of the Iraqi Islamic Party (IIP) to provincial offices, including the governor, Mamoun al-Alwani. The Sunni supporters of the IIP, although a minority in al Anbar, did vote. The tribes, who hated the IIP, felt even more disempowered since not even provincial offices represented their interests (General Sean MacFarland interview 11/3/2009).

CONSPIRACY THINKING AND PERCEPTIONS OF IRAN AND THE SHI'A

Conspiracy thinking often occurs when people are under stress as they search for a logical and irrefutable way to explain what has happened to them. Our interviews, and those done by the Marines in their oral history project, found a hefty supply of conspiracy thinking regarding Iran and, to a lesser extent, the United States, and their relationship with al Qaeda. Concern about Iran's intentions and the opportunity Iran was provided for growing violence in Iraq are evident throughout the following comments. There is also evident a strong and consistently repeated belief that Iran was behind al Qaeda's murderous behavior in al Anbar. The view of Iran as an enemy leads to predictable conspiratorial explanations. The following quotes demonstrate this tendency:

> *Sheikh Majed:* Al Qaeda was acting like religious authorities making things right and wrong as they wish not according to Islamic Sharia law, and it was all, all this was coming from Iran just (unintelligible) to destroy the Sunni, Sunni and Islamism.
>
> *Munther Saiegh:* The whole of al Qaeda, the guys who brought al Qaeda into Iraq and started the terrorism in Iraq, is one man, Ahmed Chalabi, had until this minute and organization with the Quds army in Iran, the first thing idea that Ahmed Chalabi had was how to destroy the Sunnis in Iran and he is, and al Qaeda as an organization, has been supported and until this minute supported by the Iranians and the man who brought them into Iraq is Ahmed Chalabi. He is the one who brought the militias and started the trouble from Iraq supported and ordered by the Iranians.
>
> *Jalal al-Gaood:* It was amazing to us, because seeing Iraq leadership and U.S. leadership promoting and supporting religious leadership from Iran to control Iraq was just, I mean, there is really no simple logic to that. Just way outside that. So to the Sunnis this was the enemy, as simple as that. Bringing these Iranians, or Iranians religious sheikhs to control the country so they're gonna fight for that.
>
> *Sheikh Sabah:* I agree with that [that the Iranians are behind al Qaeda]. From my experience, most of the weapons they used were Iranian made weapons.[2]

And show me one incident they had attack in Iran by al Qaeda. And many members of bin Laden's family are in Iran. And Zarqawi, when he was sick he went to Iran. So the Iranian support for al Qaeda is clear. AQ has different branches. There is the Iranians, there is the Syrians, and others.

Sheikh Tariq: When we start to do our research we found out the al Qaeda, the majority of them pushed from Iran, they were trying to create this kind of conflict between the American coalition and the local people, and they succeeded with that. . . . That's why many mistakes has been done . . . and the worst thing that the same people they support Iran to interfere in our situation and Iran start to inject some al Qaeda people loose in Iraq, most of them are Sunni to convince our people that the Americans that come to Iraq will occupy Iraq, not to liberate Iraq. . . .

Shiekh X: It is said there are three sections of al Qaeda, or three categories; one is true al Qaeda, which they are fighting only Americans, and there is another al Qaeda that is supported by Iran, which with the goal to do operations against the Sunnis in the Sunni areas, and there is a third al Qaeda supported by the Americans. Did you hear about this before? . . . Those are agents inside al Qaeda to reveal them and find out, so they were created by the Americans as agents to go inside al Qaeda, so they are al Qaeda inside al Qaeda so they are able to get the intelligence on one or two al Qaeda.

Sheikh Sabah: Iran was the number one in supplying the financial aid. And I can say tens of millions of dollars were supporting al Qaeda (Marine interview 2009: 145).

Although Sunni and Shi'a identities had grown and hardened in the preceding years and following the invasion, the interviewees did not automatically assume that the Iraqi Shi'a were all pro-Iranian. For example, Sheikh Sheikh Ali Hatim stated, "I had made a statement on the air that the trouble and the problems were neither the Americans nor the Iraqi government, but it was the Iranians. I also said that there is no connection between the Iranians and the Shiites of Iraq" (Marine interview, 2009: p. 115). Sheikhs Sabah and Tariq agreed:

Sheikh Sabah: There are two types of Shiites in Iraq. The Arabs, they are Iraqis and we don't doubt their patriotism. But those Shiites in the government, they are all Iranians. We don't exclude anyone, they are all Iranians.

Sheikh Tariq: But at the same time there are many Shi'a nationalists who didn't leave Iraq, and because of these people and their power the other nationalist Shi'a, they cannot be on the leader stage. They are avoided because they are against Iran. I can tell you I am very confident that there are many nationalist Shi'a that are more than near other people other Iraqi people that are nationalists, but they don't have the possibility to do something, to do the change.

In these comments it is clear that they make a distinction between Iraqi nationalist Shi'a who are loyal to Iraq (though not the same as the Sunni identity which they view as synonymous with Iraqi identity as discussed previously) and those who serve in the Maliki government. They consider those Shi'a working in the Maliki government as "Iranian" and disloyal to Iraqi national interests.

EARLY SIGNS OF REVOLT: AL QAIM

Facing the rising AQI attacks on the one side, a growingly aggressive US occupational force on the other, and yet another flank facing the perceived threat of an Iranian-led domestic political movement, the Sunnis of al Anbar lived in a tremendously threatening environment by late 2004. Sheikh Ali Hatim recalled that he and others met with the Ministers of Defense and Interior in 2005 asking for permission to form a militia with 2,500 fighters to protect the "western desert" (Marine interview, 2009: 108). Permission was granted, but they could not recruit the necessary fighters because their fear of al Qaeda was too great. People in the al Anbar region hunkered down in the midst of engulfing threats and escalating violence.

The First Revolt against al Qaeda

The Albu Mahal tribe resides in the al Qaim area, close to the Syrian border. This tribe lives along the Euphrates River stretching above and below al Qaim. They also have tribal members in Hit and Qubaisa (Todd, 2006: 4/27). The city itself is 250 miles northwest of Baghdad on the Euphrates. The Albu Mahal tribal members were not initial supporters of the insurgency that followed the overthrow of Saddam Hussein (Todd, 2006). But after the Americans replaced the British in their area, and for reasons discussed previously, they became increasing hostile toward the Americans. Over time following the American replacements, support for the insurgency increased among the population in the region. According to Sheikh Sabah, the principal sheikh of the Albu Mahal, the Americans had little experience with Iraqis, and resorted to excessive violence in dealing with people. He stated, "the Americans in that area were just murderers. They did not distinguish between normal citizen, terrorist, they just dealt with everyone the same way" (interview 3/10/2010). Support for the insurgents was scattered, and did not extend to the tribe's leaders. Todd argues that the tribe began to support insurgents, including al Qaeda, because of the general lack of security in the area. Neither the US nor the Iraqi government provided forces to provide security in al Qaim (2006). Meanwhile, other tribes in the area, including both the Karabila and Salmoni, gave broader support to al Qaeda.

By the end of 2004, Sheikh Sabah and the Albu Mahal tribe had had enough of al Qaeda's Taliban-style rule and violence. In April 2005, the tribe's leaders asked for help from the Iraqi government and the Americans, but the request was rejected. US forces, 1MEF, did launch an attack on al Qaeda along the Syrian border in May, 2005, called Operation Matador. Although they killed 125 al Qaeda fighters, they did not coordinate with the tribes, several tribal members were also killed (Todd, 2006: 4/33; Perry, 2010: 100). There were low-level conflicts between the tribe and al Qaeda until May, 2005, when the fighting escalated after the chief of police was assassinated by al Qaeda, and AQI declared al Qaim the Islamic State of Iraq (Sabah interview, 3/10/2010; Marine interview with Sabah, 2009:141). At this point, Sheikh Sabah recalled, "we started to understand their mission was to destroy our tribe" (Marine interview, 2009: 141).

Despite having few arms, and a reduced number of fighters, because many tribal members were in American custody, according to Sheikh Sabah, the tribe managed to drive al Qaeda out of the cities and villages, but they remained in the surrounding areas. Al Qaeda requested permission to return, which the Sheikh rejected (Marine interview, 2009: 142). More fighting ensued in August, 2005, again initiated by an assassination. Al Qaeda arrested and then killed the governor, who was a cousin of Sheikh Sabah (Marine interview, 2009: 142). This time al Qaeda managed to defeat the tribe's forces (Sabah, Marine interview, 2009, 142). Sabah stated that al Qaeda had 4,000 troops in the August fighting, and that they engaged in guerrilla warfare. The fighting in the summer of 2005 was also inter-tribal. The Albu Mahal clashed with the two tribes that supported al Qaeda, the Karabila and Salmani. This "led to months of vicious tribal feuding, including reports of beheadings and regular gun battles" (Todd, 2006: 4/33).

Al Qaeda's defeat of the tribal militias allowed AQI to return to al Qaim in August and September, 2005. Sheikh Sabah maintains that they got no assistance from the United States. In our interview and in the Marine interview, he insisted that the Americans did nothing to help during their battles with al Qaeda, and that Americans did nothing to stop insurgents heading into al Qaim from Bayji and Mosul, even though they observed them en route (Marine interview, 2009: 142). Perry (2010), however, argues that there was American assistance. In particular, in late July, Ken Wischkaemper, a participant in the 2004 negotiations in Amman, received a call from Talal al Gaood saying that there were heavily armed al Qaeda insurgents attacking the Albu Mahal tribal militia. Wischkeamper passed the alarm along to the Marines, and within an hour Cobra attack helicopters were on their way to attack the al Qaeda insurgents (Perry, 2010: 101–102).

In any case, the tribal militia retreated. Sheikh Sabah recalled: "We started losing ground and al Qaeda were able to enter al Qaim after one week of those battles. So I phoned one of my tribal persons residing here in Amman, one of our sheikhs. So we gave the orders for the tribe to withdraw to a safe place" (Interview 3/10/2010). Sabah's next step was to regroup and organize a better fighting force. He reported:

> I phoned the Minister of Defense in Iraq. At that time it was Saddoon Dulaymi, and he came to meet me here in Amman and we met at the Royal Hotel. He asked, requested for 500 people from the tribe so I gave him the names. He requested a person to coordinate with him in Baghdad so I sent an expatriate from my tribe to coordinate with him. We have formed the Desert Protection Force. They were made of 280 people and all of them were from my tribe, the Albu Mahal. The other tribes refused to join. On the contrary, many of the tribes joined al Qaeda and they were attacking us. We had training for 2 months. They were equipped with arms and vehicles. We asked the military also to help them in the battles. We were able to fight against AQ and free the area from AQ and it went back under the authority of the government by the end of October 2005. Until today al Qaim is still under authority of the government. (Interview 3/10/2010)

By the fall of 2005, the Desert Protection Force (also referred to as the Hamza Brigade) was cooperating with American Marines fighting al Qaeda in military operations (Todd, 2006: 4/34).

Despite the successes of the Albu Mahal tribe in fighting AQI, the province continued to deteriorate. Generally, AQI continued to dominate life in al Anbar through the summer of 2006. By mid-August, 2006 1MEF reported "the daily average number of attacks exceeds 50 per day in al-Anbar province. This activity reflects a 57% increase in overall attack numbers since. . . . February [2006]" (1MEF, 2006: 1). While the Albu Mahal effort to get rid of AQI was the most dramatic, others also attempted to fight back, but with little success. Sheikh Aifan Sadun of the Albu Issa tribe reported that he publicly opposed AQI in 2005, and Sheikh Jassim Saleh of the Albu Soda tribe and his kinsman Sheikh Abdul Rahman al-Janabi worked together to resist AQI in the tribal area east of Ramadi in 2004–2005, but they did not meet with success (Marine interviews, 2009).

Nevertheless, the rumblings among the sheikhs who remained in al Anbar increased. The al Qaim events seem to have provided encouragement to talks already taking place in Anbar. Kairy Hekmayen, a businessman from al Anbar, stated that discussions regarding an Awakening began as early as 2005 (Interview, 3/16/2010). There were continuing efforts on the diplomatic side to promote collaboration between the Americans and the Sunni tribes to stabilize al Anbar. US ambassador to Iraq, Zalmay Khalilzad, met with Talal al Gaood and discussed a recommendation by the Iraq Initiative for Unity and Development regarding economic matters. James Clad and General Hamdani developed a proposal called "Winning Iraq, One City at a Time" (Perry, 2010: 103). Finally, a meeting was held between US Army officers and Sunni sheikhs in Ramadi in November 2005 where ideas similar to those discussed in 2004 were proposed, involving Sunni collaboration with the Americans to rid al Anbar of insurgents (Perry, 2010). Unfortunately, enhanced cooperation between the Americans and the Sunni tribes remained elusive for nearly a year.

Talks among the tribal leaders continued, however, and there were increasing signs of collaboration in late 2005 and into the spring and summer of 2006. Sheikh Aakab al Good recalled the formation of a militia called the Anbar Rebels in 2006, which was a small force that dressed like AQI forces and conducted assassinations of AQ leaders.[3] The success of this militia gave encouragement to the resistance to AQI (interview 2/15/2010; see also Marine interview with Sheikh Ali Hatim, 2009). The militia fighters were probably former nationalist insurgents who had realigned with the tribes (General MacFarland interview 11/3/2009). In another example of growing collaboration among the tribes, the Anbar Peoples' Committee (APC) was formed in December 2005, which consisted of sheikhs from twelve Anbari tribes, with the goal of organizing resistance to AQI. The APC was organized by Sheikh Nasser al Fahdawi of the Albu Fahad tribe and Mohammed Mahmoud Latif, who was a religious leader (Micheals, 2010). It did not last long, as General Allen explained (Interview 12/9/2009).

> In early '06 [late 2005] the tribes around Ramadi formed the Anbar Peoples' Committee [Council], with about 11 medium to small sized tribes. The philosophical trajectory of the APC wasn't an alliance narrative with the Coalition. They hadn't yet decided that their bread was better buttered on our side than on AQ's side. AQ had a liberation narrative: Saddam is gone, the Americans are the occupiers, the Americans have destroyed your society as you know it, we AQ will join with the native resistance and we will eject the Americans. So they had a pretty powerful narrative. It wasn't until you embraced AQ that you realized you had embraced a medieval Salafist system of Islam that generally was very different than the way the tribes lived, which was a very moderate, semi-modern approach. So the Anbar People's Committee formed, AQ recognized it for what it was, which was the very first time there appeared to be an organized resistance to them at the tribal level, and they couldn't tolerate it.

AQI signaled their opposition to the Anbar People's Committee on January 5, 2006, with a suicide bombing at a police recruitment site, an old glass factory. The recruitment program had been going very well, which signaled approval by the APC, even though they had not openly approved of cooperation with the Americans. After four days of accelerating numbers of volunteers showing up for police recruitment, AQI struck with a suicide bomber killing over fifty Iraqis (Michaels, 2010: 101). Sheikh Nasser was assassinated soon after. They continued with a consistent campaign of murder and intimidation, and successfully destroyed the effort to resist them. As General Allen explained:

> They [AQI] counter-attacked pretty quickly. . . . They killed 5 or 6 of the sheikhs, in some cases including the entire families. That is pretty hard to do in a tribal society, these are big families, but in some cases the sheikh and his immediate family were completely wiped out. The attempt by AQ was to make an example. So what's happening is more and more of these tribes are under pressure by AQ, the Anbar People's Committee, which seemed to be a good idea for everybody, was decimated by AQ and the criminality of the AQ syndicate is really siphoning off the resources of the tribes. Pretty quickly you're beginning to see the sheikhs wonder about the survival of the tribal system writ-large and their own tribes in particular. (Interview 12/9/2009)

Meanwhile, Sheikh Faisal al Gaood, the father of Sheikh Aakab al Gaood, was endeavoring to bring tribal sheikhs together. His top aid was Sheikh Hamid al Hais, a member of the Iraq Salvation Council.[4]Al Hais's tribe, the Albu Dyab, had started to fight against AQI along with the Albu Ali Jassem in the al Jazeera area of Ramadi. Al Gaood's tribe, the Albu Nimr, started to move toward Hit to combat an insurgent group linked to AQI, the Ansar al Sunna.

The fighting between the nationalist insurgents who had aligned with the tribes in January and February 2006 in the Ramadi area was very costly to the tribes. They lost badly to AQI (MacFarland interview 11/3/2009). Nevertheless, the sheikhs continued to negotiate. A central issue was whether and how to approach the Americans. Some sheikhs were wary; others had developed relationships with the Americans, but could pay a heavy price for cooperating with them. Sheikh Ali Jassem, for example, actively recruited tribal sons to join the police force. He was assassinated in August 2006 while in the process of trying to convince other sheikhs to encourage recruiting for the police forces. AQI hid his body in the desert for days, preventing its burial in accordance with Muslim traditions within one day of death. This act was viewed as an egregious disrespect for Muslim tradition and attack on tribal prestige, which proved to be a serious strategic mistake on AQI's part. It mobilized tribal resistance, which had already been developing over the summer of 2006 (MacFarland interview, 11/3/2009). These events also helped crystallize the tribal perception of AQI as a barbarian, with a low culture and low regard for important religious and cultural norms. This solidifying image further accelerated the drive for cooperation between tribes despite the growing risks. Atrocities continued in the region as Sheikh Khalid Araq al-Ataymi was also killed, his head severed and his body left in a street for three days (Sheikh

Wissam, Marine interview, 2009: 55). Sheikh Sattar of the Albu Risha tribe also cooperated with the Americans and it was well known that associating with him was dangerous. As Sheikh Wissam explained, "it was hard for the tribal people to come into Abu Risha's compound because he was considered an agent of the Americans. When I sent for groups to come in, a lot of times, out of four you may get two killed on the road" (Marine interview, 2009: 55).

The sheikhs faced additional problems while developing their plans for a revolution against AQI. One was getting support from the sheikhs in exile. As mentioned earlier, in AQI's attempt to displace the al Anbar tribal leadership and power in the region, the top-ranked sheikhs were early targets of AQI and many had gone into exile in Jordan, Syria, or Saudi Arabia for security. This disrupted the traditional tribal decision-making system. The lower-ranked sheikhs left in al Anbar had to react quickly to developments on the ground. Communication with the sheikhs outside of Anbar of necessity would be more general and strategic than immediate and tactical. Sheikh Wissam described the reaction of the exiled sheikhs to the developing plans for a revolt against AQI:

> We let it be known that 90 percent of the tribal sheikhs were in Jordan. From over there, from abroad, we faced stiff resistance to the initiation of a counter terrorism undertaking. They accused us of trying to take over the tribes, trying to be sheikhs. They said, "You are not sheikhs. You cannot do this. You cannot do that." They mocked us. They said, "You're trying to take on al-Qaeda—the ones who fought America?" They laughed at us. They said "You people are simple-minded. You cannot do what you think you're going to do." (Marine interview, 2009: 56)

Wissam's statement is probably an exaggeration. The sheikhs in exile maintain that they were in constant communication with the junior sheikhs in al Anbar (Sheikh Majed interview 3/6/2010). As one interviewee noted, if the paramount sheikhs had been against the movement that developed into the Awakening, it would have collapsed. Their silence was enough of a tacit approval (A. Khirbit interview, 3/22/2010).

Tribal leaders from Ramadi and other parts of al Anbar held meetings in July to discuss the situation, and were already considering approaching the American forces in search of a cooperative effort against AQI. It is likely that a significant amount of distrust of the Americans existed at this time. Nevertheless, they gradually moved toward an agreement that cooperating with the Americans was the best way to eliminate AQI from al Anbar. The Americans had weapons, resources, and the capacity to train a new Iraqi security force. Discussions during the summer of 2006 would lead to the formal pronouncement of the Awakening.

There are differences of opinion as to who actually "started" the Awakening. The son of Sheikh Faisal al Gaood claims his father came up with the idea in 2006 (Interview, Aakab al Gaood 3/15/2010). Sheikh Sattar was killed in 2007, but his brother, Sheikh Ahmad Albu Risha, maintains in a written response to questions that the tribes responded positively to "the invitation of the martyr Sheikh Abdul Sattar Abu Risha to form a field command made of the elite group of the sons of those tribes who have the expertise and experience of combat in order to organize the ranks and mobilize to deal with al Qaeda and the rest of the crime gangs" (Written communication received 3/20/2010).

Although Sheikh Sattar Albu Risha emerged as the most notable leader of the Awakening, Faisal al-Gaood, Hamid al Hais, Ali Hatim, Wissam al-Aethawi, and several others were among the important figures in the Awakening. Sattar's position was unusual for a number of reasons. His was a small tribe in the second or third tier of the tribal hierarchy (General Allen, interview). The tribe had a reputation for gangsterism, and Sattar himself was regarded by many as a thug. Munther Saiegh explains Sattar's emergence as the leader of the Awakening as follows:

> And the heads said, that as the head of the tribe we cannot fight, we do not show ourselves to the fighters because we are not the fighters, we have to be a gangster just like the terrorist to fight them, and the only one who was against it from the whole of al Anbar at the time was Abdul Sattar Albu Risha, so for being a gangster to fight against us that would be fine, and we know his history and they had to appoint someone as ruthless as Abdul Sattar Albu Risha to start fighting . . . and that how it becomes Abdul Sattar Albu Risha the head of the Awakening. (Interview 3/6/2010)

Albu Risha's tribe turned against AQI early on for various reasons. The Albu Risha's principal sheikh, Sattar's father, and two brothers had been killed by AQI in the preceding years. AQI also interfered with the tribe's ability to maintain economic and revenue-generating operations such as smuggling. This case illustrates the dual resource competition and identity-based conflict between the tribes and AQI. Once it became established in the region, AQI took over this lucrative activity for their own purposes, and when Sattar's father, Sheikh Bazi al-Rishawi complained, he was killed (Kukis, 2006). This proved to be yet another strategic blunder on the part of AQI. In July 2006, Sheikh Sattar agreed to provide recruits from his tribe for the police, who would be trained, armed, and paid by the United States (Deane, 2010: 85).

In sum, by the summer of 2006, one vector in the Awakening was forming on the tribal side. They began to fear for the existence of the tribal system, a fundamental existential threat to their social identity. In the events prior to the invasion of 2003, AQI had transformed from a force that would liberate them from the Americans, and presumably restore their power, to one that threatened to destroy their social identity. It had transitioned from an image of an ally to an image of a barbarian as the tribes experienced increasing atrocities at the hands of a power- and resource-seeking AQI. At the same time that this perception shifted, their perceptions of the Americans began to change as well. The image the Sunni tribal leaders held of the Americans had already transitioned from that of a benevolent imperial to an exploitative imperial. Yet the image shift was not yet complete, as it began in this time to shift from that of the imperialist to a prospective ally against AQI. We turn now to the development of the other vector, the American change in strategy.

THE AMERICANS CHANGE STRATEGY

In previous chapters we noted the absence of a counterinsurgency doctrine in military planning, as well as a refusal to recognize the development of an insurgency in Iraq at the civilian level. Instead, the plan put forth by the Joint Forces Command was a comprehensive campaign that assumed that the various subcommands would play a coordinated role in military operations against an enemy similarly organized (Andres, 2010). The central goal after the defeat of the Iraqi Army was to kill or capture "enemies of the legitimate government of Iraq," Rumsfled's euphemism for insurgents (Packer, 2006). As discussed, there was no "Phase IV" guidance for what to do after the defeat of the Iraqi military, which would have involved political and economic programs, as well as the establishment of Iraqi security forces. This forced improvisation by military commanders, producing a wide variation of actual conduct of American forces. In addition to the doctrinal problem, there was a great deal of transition in the military command. The Combined Joint Task Force (CJTF) took control of operations in Iraq and reported to CENTCOM. General Franks, who led the invasion, retired and was replaced by General John Abizaid as head of CENTCOM in July 2003. General William Wallace, V Corps commander and the tactical commander for American forces in Iraq, was replaced by General Ricardo Sanchez on June 14, 2003, and the next day V Corps became the Combined Joint Task Force 7 (CJTF-7) responsible for tactical and strategic operations (Andres, 2010). CJTF-7 created a campaign plan, which was published in January 2004, that allowed greater flexibility for local commands, so that they could adapt to local conditions, but this was contrary to the joint doctrine (Andres, 2010). The result was confusion. Marine Colonel T.X. Hammes described it as "Each division was operating so differently, right next to the other—absolutely hard-ass here, and hearts-and-minds here" (quoted in Packer, 2006: 4). The diversity in approaches created confusion and inconsistency in policies toward Sunni tribes, and added to the general disarray and threat environment in the province.

In January 2004, Multinational Corps–Iraq (MNC-I) replaced CJTF-7 and took over responsibilities for "tactical and operational headquarters in Iraq" (Andres, 2010: 46). In July, 2004, Mulitnational Force–Iraq (MNF-I) was created to provide advice to MNC-I regarding strategy. They developed a strategy issued in November, 2004, but by then the insurgency was full blown. In al Anbar during this time, Major Ben Connable recalled, the Americans were engaging with the tribes, promising them help in exchange for their cooperation against the growing insurgency. However,

> We promised a great many things, and of course we couldn't deliver them. And we demanded of them a quid pro quo. . . . We never got the fact that we were asking something from somebody who was incapable of delivering it. . . . It was foolish on our part to assume that we were going to make any progress in the absence of stability. . . . So, of course in '04 we had done almost nothing to establish security. I argue that we had insufficient troop-to-task from day one. We did not really appreciate the complexity of the insurgency, the number of different groups, the motivation of the insurgents themselves. (Marine interview 2009: 122–123)

Connable also maintains that the United States lost a golden opportunity in late 2005 when the tribes started to fight against AQI and formed the Anbar People's Counsel. Instead of providing more troops for the province after the relative success of the December 2005 elections, General George W. Casey announced that the next two brigades scheduled for deployment in Iraq were going to be held in reserve. Had that not happened, the United States could have provided more security in al Anbar, and the Anbar People's Counsel, already geared up to fight AQI, could have joined forces with the United States (Marine interview, 2009: 128–129). Instead, AQI regrouped and quickly killed off half of the founders of the Anbar People's Counsel.

Nevertheless, counterinsurgency ideas began to take hold in military planning and training.[5] Then-Colonel H.R. McMaster, for example, along with other officers in Fort Carson Colorado, trained his men in the 3rd Armored Cavalry Regiment to understand Iraqi culture and a variety of likely scenarios they would face when they were deployed in Tal Afar. Soldiers were trained to sit down with people, several times, engaging in social niceties and drinking tea, in an effort to gather intelligence from them as a preferred strategy rather than kicking in doors and throwing them to the floor. In short, McMaster was taking seriously the complaints and grievances expressed by the people of al Anbar. McMaster ordered his soldiers "never to swear in front of Iraqis or call them 'hajjis' in a derogatory way (this war's version of 'gook')" (Packer, 2006: 4). In the process they learned to empathize with the Iraqis, humanize them, and to listen to them. The model image of the Sunnis began to change from that of a rogue to an ally, at least at the level of the military officers who took the lead in implementing a counterinsurgency strategy. It is reflected in the following quotes:

Remarking on the value of a cultural training course at Fort Carson, Colorado, Packer (2006) quotes Captain Sellars:

> Sellars told me, "I don't know how many times I've thought, and then heard others say, 'Wish I'd known that the first time." The rehearsals [of potential scenarios interacting with Iraqis] in Colorado, he said, amounted to a recognition that "this war is for the people of Iraq." Sellars . . . described it as a kind of training in empathy. "Given these circumstances, what would be my reaction?" he asked. "If I was in a situation where my neighbor had gotten his head cut off, how would I react? If it was my kid that had gotten killed by mortars, how would I react?"

The quote illustrates a recognition of equality as people, and the complexity of the other, both signs of the ally image. No longer is the other seen in simplified terms and as one to be punished or crushed in order to instill obedience and desired behavior. Rather, the complexity and contextual realities of the other's situation are recognized, and engagement with those realities is recognized as the best way to meet potentially mutually desired ends. The ideas of equality and a recognition of opportunities for engagement without the use of brute force and threat motivation are reflected in the following statements by Colonel Tony Deane and General MacFarland:

> You could talk with them man to man. They are businessmen, reasonable people. (Deane interview 11/10/2009).

> I went out to one of these temporary Iraq police stations that we had set up where the Sheikhs wanted them. And interestingly most of them were right across the street from a sheikh's house, but that's ok it worked for them. I didn't care, if that's what works. And it did. It didn't seem to make sense to my western military mind, but it made sense to them and that was what was important. (MacFarland, interview 11/3/2009)

The capability of the tribes, another component of the ally image, is evident in this statement by General MacFarland:

> They [his superiors] said you know these guys [the sheikhs] have their strange ways of doing things, you got to keep them at arms' length, we don't trust them. And I said you gotta be careful, I understand that, but you cannot do counterinsurgency without dealing with sheikhs. If you do that it's like trying to swim the English channel without getting wet. (Interview 11/3/2009)

These quotes differ from the quotes representing the rogue image in important ways. The ally image is associated with a respect for the leadership and context of particular political settings in which the perceived actor operates. The rogue image is associated with an assumption, a requirement, that the perceived obey the instruction of the perceiver. There is an assumption that the rogue "doesn't know any better" and has to be led, commanded, and disciplined. These aforementioned quotes illustrate a very different perception of the Sunni leadership—a perception that the leadership is operating in a context that is complex and not fully understood by the observer, and that there must be a good reason for the decisions being made. There is an important aspect of the assumptions of motivation in this ally image as well, that is different from the rogue image. There is an assumption that the motivations for the decisions are good, even if the logic isn't even understood. Those perceived as an ally get the benefit of doubt.

IMPLEMENTING THE NEW STRATEGY

Colonel McMaster got the opportunity to implement the new strategy when he took the 3rd ACR to Tal Afar in northwestern Iraq in 2005. Tal Afar was extremely violent with sectarian divisions between the Shi'a and Sunni and a strong presence of insurgents. It was a transit point for insurgents coming into Iraq from Syria and "central to the strategy of Abu Musab al-Zarqawi" who "exploited tribal and sectarian divisions among the city's poor and semiliterate population" (Packer, 2006: 5). McMaster and his subordinates fought their way into the city, but instead of destroying it, they studied the local power dynamics, talked with tribal sheikhs, offered security, offered contracts for economic development projects, and began to recruit men into the police. This approach proved to be slow and time consuming, but they were successful in forging strong ties with the tribes. The 3rd ACR began recruiting men into the police force and they began awarding contracts for economic development projects. The results were slow and steady progress in driving the insurgents out of the area and a burgeoning trust between the tribes and the US forces in the area. This approach became a template for future operations.

Zarqawi was furious about the American successes in Tal Afar. He gave a speech condemning the Americans (crusaders), and the Shiites (Rafidites) and accused both of mass slaughter of Sunnis:

> This battle has come in order to unveil the ugly face of the government of the descendants of Ibn Al-'Alqami and to remove the shield behind which they hide. The Rafidite neighborhoods [in Tel'afar] have been isolated in order to

> spare them from the bombings and destruction, and in order to use some of them to launch a war of total annihilation on the Sunni neighborhoods, as a step toward eliminating any sign of life in those neighborhoods. It has been proven to us beyond a shadow of a doubt that the Crusaders are using toxic gases in their battles against the mujahideen, even if the masters of the Black [i.e. White] House and their followers deny it. Ask the hospitals of Tel'afar about the widespread cases of asphyxiation and poisoning among those admitted there. . . .
>
> Finally, we say to the Crusaders and the Safavid Rafidites: Your crime and cowardly deed at Tel'afar will not go without severe punishment, Allah willing. I challenge the government of the descendants of Ibn Al-'Alqami, headed by Al-Ja'fari the Zoroastrian and 'Abu Righal' Al-Dulaimi, to come out of their lairs in the Green Zone [in Baghdad], and to confront the brigades of the mujahideen. (al-Zarqawi, 2005)

The significance of Tal Afar for al Anbar is that it was a training ground for some of the officers who moved to al Anbar in May, 2006. In particular, then-Colonel Sean MacFarland, commander of the 1st Brigade Combat Team, 1st Armored Division (1/1 AD), the Ready First Brigade, operated in Tal Afar before moving to Ramadi in al Anbar in late May, 2006. He had previously served in the CJTF-7 in Baghdad. In Ramadi, the 1/1 AD was subordinate to the First Marine Expeditionary Force (1MEF), which had replaced the 82nd Airborne Division and 3rd Armored Cavalry Regiment in al Anbar in January 2004. MacFarland's new boss was Marine Major General Richard Zilmer. MacFarland was fully familiar with the grass-roots counterinsurgency program in Tal Afar, and he brought with him junior officers with similar experience. The 1/1AD was joined by the "1st Battalion, 35th Armor (Task Force Conqueror); 1st Battalion, 37th Armor (Task Force Bandit); 2d Battalion (-); 501st Forward Support Battalion (501st FSB); 1st Battalion, 506th Infantry (Task Force Currahee); 3d Battalion, 8th Marine Regiment (3/8 Marines); a detachment of U.S. Navy Seals; and other enablers that were already in place in Ramadi" (Deane, 2010: 81). They replaced a National Guard brigade from Pennsylvania.

Even before the arrival of the new forces into al Anbar, General Zilmer began operational planning for securing Ramadi. Then-Major Ben Connable, who took part in the planning, states that the operation was going to go ahead with or without the tribes. "We realized at that point that the tribes were not ready. There were very few tribal leaders . . . that had the ability to do any positive coercion, because again, tribal members were not ready to do anything positive. . . . So, at that point it was essentially a coalition effort to establish security. Now, we included our Iraqi partners in that. The Iraqi army was going to play a very big role in helping to secure Ramadi" (Marine interview 2009: 131).

When MacFarland arrived in Ramadi, the situation was dire. Smith and MacFarland described Ramadi as follows:

> In the summer of 2006, Ramadi by any measure was among the most dangerous cities in Iraq. The area of operations averaged over three times more attacks per capita than any other area in the country. With the exception of the embattled government center and nearby buildings held by a company of Marines, Al-Qaeda-related insurgents had almost complete freedom of movement throughout the city. They dominated nearly all of the city's key structures, including the city hospital, the largest in Anbar Province. Their freedom of movement allowed them to emplace complex subsurface IED belts, which rendered much of the city no-go terrain for U.S. and Iraqi Army (AI) forces. (Smith & MacFarland, 2008: 41–42)

Al Qaeda had declared Ramadi the capital of the future caliphate in Iraq and there were no security forces to speak of in Ramadi (Smith & MacFarland, 2008; Deane, 2010).

The first task of the American forces was to take the city of Ramadi back. They entered the city with tanks, which gave the citizens and the insurgents the impression that they were going to initiate a battle like that for Fallujah, although MacFarland's orders were to take back the city, "but don't make it another Fallujah" (Deane, 2010: 81). When they arrived they faced attacks by "bombs, grenades, mortars, and rifle fire, an average of 25 times a day" (Ricks, 2009: 62). The Americans quickly established combat outposts (COPs) around and then inside the city. The plan was to develop smaller combat outposts rather than staying in larger forward operating bases (FOBs) as the US military did previously. The initial military strategy was designed to "clear, hold, and build," that is, drive AQI out and create an increasingly secure environment for the citizens of Ramadi, one neighborhood at a time (Deane, 2010; Smith & MacFarland, 2008). They intended to do what they could not do in 2004: provide the initial security that was necessary to get cooperation from the tribes. During this time, force size forced close cooperation with the Iraqi Security Forces, both Army and police. These units were, as mentioned, targets of AQI attack, and the Americans "immediately began investing in the Iraqi Security Forces" with military transition teams (Deane, 2010: 82). Members of these teams would stay with the Iraqi Army at checkpoints and on patrols. American and Iraqi soldiers lived together at the COPs, which improved everything from cultural understanding to weapons maintenance (Ricks, 2009). The Americans mentored the Iraqis, but this also gave the Iraqi Army a presence and provided evidence to the populace that Iraqis were fighting against AQI and that the battle was not simply an American one.

A second part of the American strategy was to rebuild the Iraqi Police. Smith and MacFarland write that the experience in Tal Afar taught them the importance of competent police forces in maintaining success against AQI. The American and Iraqi Army may be able to beat them, but keeping them at bay required a reliable police force (2008). In Ramadi, the police had 420 officers in June, 2006, out of an authorization of 3,386 officers. Of those 420, fewer than 140 actually went to work, and most days had fewer than 100 on duty (Smith & MacFarland, 2008: 44). They also understood that the only way to recruit men into the police was to get collaboration from the sheikhs. In a tribal society, there would be no volunteers unless the sheikhs encouraged their tribal "sons" to volunteer. In order to get their cooperation, sheikhs predisposed to work with the Americans had to be identified, and they had to have a major incentive: the assurance that their own security would be protected.

Getting the necessary cooperation from the tribes was problematic when MacFarland's unit arrived. The military's calculation was that only six of the twenty-one tribes in the area would work with the US forces (Ricks, 2009: 63). The Bezia family of the Albu Risha tribe, Sheikh Sattar's family, was openly supportive of the Americans. As mentioned, one way to promote cooperation was to provide for the personal security of tribal sheikhs. This was done by placing tanks at intersections near their compounds, and by soliciting their advice as to where to put new police stations (Ricks, 2009; MacFarland, interview 11/3/2009). The sheikhs who cooperated would get police stations near their compounds, which pushed AQI into the neighborhoods of those who did not cooperate (MacFarland, interview 11/3/2009). In addition, by placing policemen in stations in their own tribe's territory, the police officers had a greater incentive to protect and to become "hunters" of insurgents (Smith & MacFarland, 2010: 47). The first recruiting drive backed by the Albu Rishas occurred on July 4, 2006, at the Bezia family compound (Deane, 2010). Recruitment continued through the summer of 2006, and those who passed the induction process were sent to the Police Training Academy in Amman, Jordan (Deane, 2010).

The new American strategy reenergized the tribal determination to resist AQI, and the change in American behavior promoted some improvement in the perception and trust in the Americans. Sheikh Tariq, for example, recalled that:

> With the arrival of the Marines in Anbar, they were ready to listen to us. That's why we start to talk to them directly and it wasn't that easy for us to take this responsibility because we know if we do not succeed our people, they will consider that we work against them with the Americans. But it was a very smart move and we start very slowly slowly and was secret at the beginning, then we start to invite this sheikh, that sheikh. (Interview 3/10/2010)

These comments indicate the impact of the changing image on the part of the American forces. The new American approach to the tribes in al Anbar created the second vector that, when joined with the first, would create the formal Awakening.

Coming Together

The new American approach of engagement with the tribes and a focus on building a police force that protected local communities began to pay off in the form of important image change among the tribal sheikhs, this time in their perception of the Americans. The changing American strategy and their efforts to reach out to the sheikhs increased their trust in the Americans and helped changed their image of the Americans from imperialists to allies. The change is reflected in the following quotes:

- This is what we did, first we established the trust [with the Americans] that's why we had many events, meetings, economic conferences. This helped the people that you are trying to help them you want to help them in the economic issues as well. . . . Not that difficult [to establish trust in the Americans] but it was hard at the beginning (Sheikh Tariq).

From these statements one can see growing confidence in and trust for the Americans, after first being greatly disappointed in American choices regarding the post–Saddam regime leadership.

- Because the Americans supported the tribal leaders during the Awakening, some trust has been build and this has changed because the Americans have started to respect and work with the tribal leaders. All the meetings, this came late, it should have come sooner (Sheikh X).
- When they [the Americans] got here they are like blind, but after a while they start to understand. . . . We are getting frustrated because of Americans. They always went to the wrong places. The Americans should have established mutual trust with the Iraqis. Unfortunately the Americans did not show any signs of trust, and the Iraqis did the same. There is a saying that true words come from heart to heart and are believed by the mind. So when they don't say true things it is hard for us to believe it. . . . When they [the Americans] entered Iraq they were enemy number one but by the time passing they became enemy number four after AQ, the Shi'a, Ministry of defense and Interior, and Iran. . . . Maybe with more time they will be number eight or nine. Maybe in the end people will understand that. (M. Hamdani)

Hamdani's remarks show both ambivalence about Americans and an improvement in his view of them as more trustworthy.

- In response to the question of whether the view of the Americans had become more positive once the Americans started supporting the Awakening. . . . Yes. Positive change, yes definitely. Because for the first time they committed to something. And people would tell you that the Americans would do this, Americans would do that, and actually they had a lot of ideas they did not. . . . For the first time they really committed themselves to something. (Khirbit)

- The Americans supported us very strongly through the projects they put in our areas, and also through the police and the Iraqi army, which we started with them and the Americans trained. (Shiekh Aifan, Marine interview, 2009: 94)
- The government of Iraq, Nouri al-Maliki called me the "American sheikh." They know I have very strong relationships with the Americans, which makes me happy. I don't feel ashamed of it. I used my friendship with the Americans to build a secure Iraq. This is what we have achieved, because it's God's wish, and with his blessing and the work between us and the Americans. (Sheikh Aifan, Marine interview 2009: p. 101)
- To tell you the truth, if you look at the Americans' role, and what they did in here, they were more interested in the welfare of the Iraqi people than the government of Anbar was. Tell you some facts—the way they stood behind us, the way they supported us, the way they kept over watch on the police apparatus. . . . So the Americans kept watch over everybody, and anybody. They kept everybody in line, and if it weren't for them, it was chaos. (Sheikh Ali Hatim, Marine interview 2009: 116)
- We became so friendly with the Americans things changed and the Americans were participating in people's weddings and happy occasions. Even when the Americans came to arrest someone the people were happy with it because it's not AQ arresting the person and it's not the government in Baghdad. (Sheikh Shouka, 3/17/2010)

These quotes are just a few examples encountered in our interviews and those conducted by the Marines in 2009, but they illustrate both the complexity of the Iraqi assessment of the Americans and the change from a negative view to the idea that it was possible to work together with the Americans, that they can rely on the Americans, and that American intentions are good, rather than threatening to Sunni tribal and Iraqi national interests. Despite these tendencies identified in the interviews, there remained concerns that the United States was primarily self-interested and that it would pull out when the time was right for the United States, not necessarily for the people of Anbar. Along with this opinion is an underlying assumption that the Americans can do anything they want, and that Iraqis' own ability to influence American policy is limited. Nevertheless, despite these changes in perception on behalf of the tribes, the changing perceptions could not immediately result in cooperation with the Americans. It continued to be dangerous to be seen talking to the Americans, and the sheikhs did not want to be accused of being American puppets.

MOVING TOWARD AN AWAKENING

As mentioned above, there is disagreement about who exactly started the Awakening. It is evident, however, that the idea of revolting against AQI was not the product of one individual or organization. One advocate of an Awakening was the Anbar Salvation Council, led by Sheikh Faisal al Gaood. The other was the tribes of Ramadi, who were pulled together by Sheikh Satter Albu Risha (written communication with Sheikh Ahmad Albu Risha, 3/20/2010). Sheikh Aifan Sadun, for example, recalled being contacted by Sheikh Sattar who suggested they join forces to fight AQI as did Sheikh Wissam (Marine interviews, 2009). Several interviewees noted that it was dangerous to meet at Sheikh Sattar's compound, because he was a target of AQI due to his close relationship with the Americans (e.g., Marine interviews with Sheikhs Wissam and Sadun Sadun, 2009). Nevertheless, Sheikh Aakab al-Gaood explains that his father, leader of the Anbar Salvation Council, wanted to meet at Sattar's home because it was *safe* due to his close relationship with the Americans. He claims the idea of a revolt was news to Sattar:

> At that point in time Sattar did not know anything about this project although he was enjoying great relations with the Americans. So my father nominated a committee including Hamid al Hais to meet with Albu Risha and explain the idea to him. Albu Risha welcomed the idea. Albu Risha himself was a target for AQ. They had successfully killed his father and other relatives as well. So Albu Risha agreed to have the conference at his house which was secured by the American forces. So that declaration found a great welcome especially in that area where it started, and lots of support from Sheikh Albu Sattar. They started coordinating and inviting other tribal leaders to support them. (Aakab al Gaood interview 3/15/2010)

Whoever came up with the idea, the discussions among the sheikhs were noted by civil affairs officer Captain Travis Patriquin, who spoke Arabic and spent a good deal of time interacting with Sheikh Sattar, visiting his compound and watching developments among the sheikhs. He kept other crucial players on the American side aware of the comings and goings of the sheikhs and alerted them to the fact that something was going on.[6] On September 2, 2006, twenty tribal leaders informed then-Lieutenant Colonel Tony Deane and Major David Raugh that they were forming an Emergency Council to eliminate AQI, and that they wanted to work with the US forces (Deane, 2010). They also informed him that they wanted the governor removed from office. The tribal sheikhs involved met on September 9, this time with Colonel MacFarland and the leadership of Task Force Conqueror. The fifty individuals at the meeting represented twenty tribes, many in full tribal regalia (MacFarland interview 11/3/2009; Ricks, 2009: 66). MacFarland described this sequence of events as follows:

> And then Sheikh Albu Risha said "Hey come on down to my house," and he basically lived right across the highway from Camp Ramadi, I mean we could see his house from one of our entry control point towers, it was within fifty kal range, and he offered to bring a lot of these sheikhs down there and talk about what we're going to do. He had lost a father and a brother and some other relatives to terrorists and he said "hey I'm, willing to come off the sidelines and be your spokesman" because everybody is afraid to be a spokesman everybody wore their masks, their balaclavas, you know because nobody wanted to be seen and Sattar said "Hey, I don't care, people know who I am, and basically I'm mad as hell and I don't want to take it anymore." . . . My battalion commander in that area said "hey sir, there's a lot of comings and goings in that area at Sattar's house." He was practically in there every day so he was kind of giving me the feedback and said "hey you need to come over and talk to this group of folks" and he told them "hey you need to talk to my brigade commander." So he kind of set this meeting up and Sheikh Sattar decided well if Colonel MacFarland is coming to my meeting I'm going to have all of my sheikhs there, you know, that want to do this. So he turned it into the big conclave sort of thing and I was a bit taken aback by the number of sheikhs there. I thought I would find 5 or 6 but depending on how you count sheikhs and who is a real sheikh there were about 20 tribes represented there and close to 40 guys in their full regalia, you know, robes, all lining the wall. . . . In the Arab way they were all lining the walls and the center was open. Down at the end there was this big love seat kind of thing. Sattar was sitting on one side of the love seat and the other side as open. That's where I was going to sit. We were the two big sheikhs at the meeting that were going to kick this thing off. (Interview, 11/3/2009)

The sheikhs produced an eleven-point document that they presented publicly on September 14. These became the tenets of the formal Awakening organization:

TENETS OF THE AWAKENING MEETING[7]

1. The return of Honorable status of Sheikhs, those Sheikhs who did not support terrorism in any way or means, to form Anbar Sheikh Council.
2. Hold Free Election among all tribes to elect the members for: Rescue Anbar Province Council, where all sons of Anbar will be democratically represented without any illegal pressures.
3. Forming of Police and Army from Anbar sons, Hiring Process and appointments should be in coordination with the sheikhs where sheikhs will issue affidavit in which they confirm the good civil conduct of the recruits from their tribes.
4. Provide security for Highway Travelers, in roads within tribal areas.
5. Condemning Terrorism wherever and whenever it is found, disclaim any attacks against CF to allow an open dialogue in order to draw a new road map for our Province.

6. Stop all arms holding in public streets, except for Police and Army.
7. Respecting the Law, supporting the judicial system, so they can uphold the Law.
8. Open dialogue with ex-Ba'athist members who have not committed any crime against Iraqis, and did not support terrorism, helping them get jobs.
9. Immediate rebuilding of agriculture, industrial development, and reopening of closed industries in order to prevent unemployment.
10. After ratification of the proclamation by tribes we will take the following action. Any person who gives refuge to any terrorist whether Arab or foreign or Iraqi shall be held responsible for his actions by his tribe Sheikh, by surrendering him to proper authorities.
11. Open dialogue with Coalition Forced in order for them to schedule withdrawal from the Anbar after complete formation of Police and Army of Anbar Province.

The list was acceptable and pleasing to the Americans. The Americans did insist that the governor could not be removed since he had been elected to office.

The sheikhs met again on September 11 and 12, planning the formal announcement of the Awakening movement on September 14 (Aakab al Gaood interview (3/15/2010). According to Aakab al Gaood, during the September 11 meeting, they decided to appoint Sheikh Sattar to be the governor of al Anbar, although this did not come to fruition. The September 14 meeting marked the emergence of a formal Sahawa organization, the Emergency Council. The leader was Sheikh Sattar, and his deputies included Hamid al Hais, who was from the Albu Dyab tribe, and Sheikh Ali Hatim, who was the nephew of the principal sheikh of the Dulaym confederation, Sheikh Majed. The Sahawa formed an Anbar Salvation Council, which went to Baghdad to get formal recognition for Prime Minister Nouri al Maliki.

CONCLUSION

In this chapter we reviewed the events leading up to the declaration that the Americans and the tribes would work together to reject AQI from al Anbar. It is a remarkable story, and we argue that it could only have resulted from a fundamental change on both the American and tribal sheikhs' part. The change was perceptual for each. The tribes began to see AQI not as a liberator, but as a barbarian determined to extinguish their social identity. The tribes also began to recognize the change in American behavior that began in Tal Afar and spread to other areas. The Americans in these areas started to become more aware that their previous approach to the tribes was contributing to instability and insecurity in the region. As a result, they slowly adopted different strategies and became much more judicial in the use of force. The American forces began to treat the Iraqis more humanely in their encounters during operations, and this produced a change in the image of the Americans from imperialist to ally. As the image theory argues, when an opponent is seen as a barbarian, the perceiver starts to look for others with whom they can ally, thereby increasing their power calculation. The tribes recognized that they could not defeat AQI without American help. As they became trustful of the Americans, they became more responsive to the image shift of seeing them as allies. The tribes at this point took the substantial risk of allying with US forces. The Americans also took the risk of allying with the tribes after recognizing that they, too, could not defeat AQI alone.

One of the most remarkable aspects of the developments leading to the Awakening was the rapidity of image change. Traditionally, it has been assumed that images are slow to change, and that even after they do change there are lingering elements of the old image in policy circles and among the public (M. Cottam, 1986). The mutual enemy images held during the cold war are examples. American and Soviet citizens and policy makers saw one another as enemies across generations, and evidence indicating that those images were misplaced, such as détente and even Gorbachev's perestroika, did not quickly disconfirm the enemy images. In al Anbar, however, images changed rapidly among Americans and the tribes. Clearly this change was reinforced by the successes against AQI that resulted from the cooperation made possible by growing perceptual change. The case also suggests yet another possible cause of bureaucratic/agency-based policy disagreements.

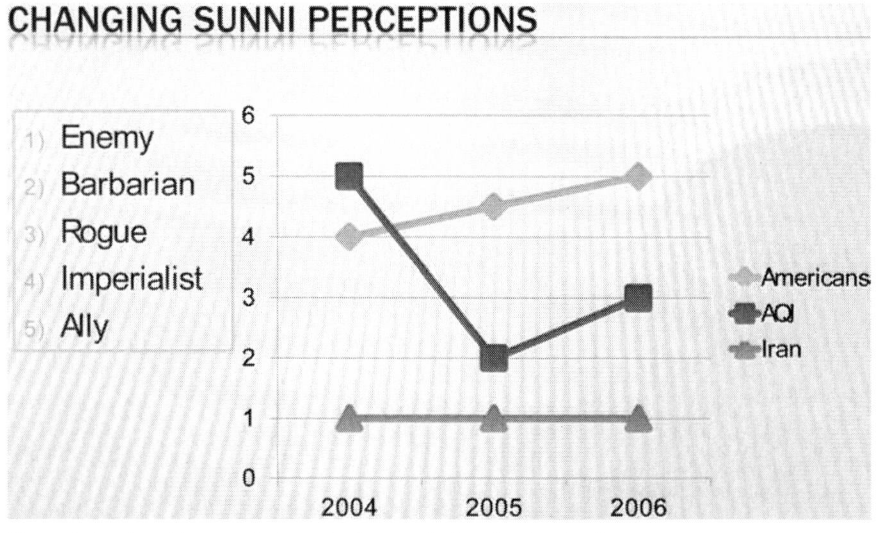

Figure 4.1 Sunni Images before, during, and after the Awakening

Those in the field, whose lives may depend on an ability to adjust their perceptions of opponents and allies, may advocate very different strategies and tactics than those safely seated in places like the Green Zone in Baghdad or Washington, D.C.

NOTES

1. They later realized that boycotting was a mistake, as it led to sound victories for the Shi'a and Kurd parties. They did not boycott the elections in December 2005, although turnout was less than 30% (Deane, 2010).
2. Iran did not give their EFP weapons to any group that was not Shi'a.
3. The Sheikh recounted that the Americans formed this militia. This was not confirmed by any of the American interviewees.
4. Sometimes translated as the Iraqi Solidarity Council.
5. The counterinsurgency doctrine, FM 3-24 *Counterinsurgency,* was published by Joint Staff J7 in December 2006, written under the direction of the Lt. General David Petraeus.
6. Many of our American interviewees credited Captain Patriquin for being instrumental in the American side of the Awakening. One went so far as to say the Awakening would not have happened without him, because he mapped the developments among the sheikhs, and made his superiors aware of them. He was killed by an IED in December, 2006.
7. This list was sent to us from BG MacFarland via COL Anthony Deane, who kept a translated copy of the document. It is also available in Deane, 2010.

Chapter 5

The Awakening Spreads

With the presentation of the formal eleven points, the formal Awakening began. General Allen made the point that the Awakening had two forms: one a formal organization, the other a principle. The principle of the Awakening occurred when the image of AQI changed for good from an ally to a barbarian, and the tribes decided that they had to resist. The formal Awakening was embodied in the Awakening Council formed after the presentation of the eleven tenets of the Awakening. The leader was Sheikh Sattar, and his deputies included Hamid al Hais who was from the Albu Dyab tribe, and Sheikh Ali Hatim, who was the nephew of the principal sheikh of the Dulaym confederation, Sheikh Majed. The Sahawa formed an Anbar Salvation Council, which went to Baghdad to get formal recognition for Prime Minister Nouri al Maliki. While Sheikh Sattar was the leader of the formal organization, he was not the leader of the Awakening movement as a whole. Sheikh Sattar was from a lower-tiered tribe, and sheikhs from other tribes who supported the Awakening movement in principal were not willing to join the organization led by Sheikh Sattar, because that would diminish their honor and status. They would listen to him politely, and often follow his suggested strategies and tactics, but they did not formally submit to him or his organization (Allen Interview 2/9/2010). As General Allen explained:

> So the other sheikhs would, if they were part of the Sahawa, they acknowledged his seniority, they acknowledged his leadership, and there were 10 tribes, 10 sheikhs, that were his supporters, and he organized them into a staff, actually. If you were not part of the Sahawa as an organization, you might well cooperate, you might well take lead from something he was doing, but you wouldn't take orders because a third tier sheikh of a second tier tribe doesn't give Sheikh Hattem of the Albu Nimrs orders. (Interview 2/9/2010)

Sheikh Sattar was clearly aware of the power of tribal politics and hierarchies and did not challenge the status and authority of tribal sheikhs who were not formal members of the Awakening organization. He told their tribesmen to obey their sheikh (A. Khirbit interview 3/22/2010).

The sheikhs wanted the Awakening movement to be recognized by the Iraqi government to give them legitimacy. A delegation from the Anbar Salvation Council[1] went to Baghdad to meet with Prime Minister Nouri al Maliki. They asked that the governor be replaced, which was denied, and that leaders who had left Anbar be appointed to official positions. The central government refused this request, arguing that those offices needed to be filled through the electoral process at the provincial level. Nevertheless, the central government did give them the "right to add nine members of the conference of the Anbar Awakening to the membership of the Anbar province governing council, in addition to the Anbar police chief and the absorption of the Awakening fighters in the national police and the military in Anbar" (Written response, Sheikh Ahmed Albu Risha's political office; A. al Gaood interview, 3/15/2010; Ahmed Albu Risha interview, Marine study, 2009). The Ministries of Defense and Interior agreed to permit those Anbaris who joined the police or army to stay in their home areas (General Allen, Interview, 2/9/2010).

Ali Hatim reports that while in Baghdad a vote was taken to determine who would lead the Anbar Salvation Council, presumably the group nominated al Hais, who won by 70 votes. Sattar then "pulled out, and he said, 'Look, I'm going with the Awakening' and here the division took place" (Marine interview 2009: 111). Ahmed Albu Risha, however, maintains that the main task of the Salvation Council was to negotiate with the central government, not lead the Awakening movement (written response). The Awakening Council was to fulfill that role. As time progressed, local Awakening Councils popped up elsewhere in al Anbar. The province-wide Council was located in Ramadi.

On the American side, a strategy was developed to get the cooperation of more and more sheikhs. This involved attacking AQI, driving it from the area and denying the AQI fighters safe havens in which to operate, thereby gaining the confidence of the Iraqi civilians through demonstrated improvement in security and military victories against AQI. This reduced the risk perceived by the tribes when deciding whether to join the Awakening. In order to achieve these strategic goals, the Americans changed the previous operational process of sending patrols from the Forward Operating Bases (FOB) outside of towns, engaging the enemy, and then returning to the FOB to the COP approach (discussed in chapter 4). Over time, the COPs disrupted AQI's ability to move among the people and enhanced the military's "ability to conduct civil-military operations; intelligence, reconnaissance and surveillance" (Smith & MacFarland, 2008: 45). In addition to training more police and building police stations near their compounds, they occasionally provided direct security to key sheikhs (Smith & MacFarland, 2008). They made "friendly sheikhs the conduits for humanitarian aid efforts, such as free fuel disbursements" (Smith & MacFarland, 2008: 43–44). They restored services, got the Ramadi General Hospital back to functional status and assured the sheikhs that they were going to stay until AQI was defeated (Smith & MacFarland, 2008). The Americans made efforts to rebuild the infrastructure, reopening roads, clearing irrigation ditches, getting the electrical grid up again, and providing seeds for farming. Contracts were also awarded to tribes for various enterprises. This was part of a broader effort to build up the power of the sheikhs, thus encouraging more to join in with the Awakening. Many of the sheikhs had construction companies with varying degrees of legitimacy, and they were eager for the contracts. Contrary to the cynical interpretation, these contracts were not awarded to "buy" cooperation from the sheikhs (Col. Tien, interview 12/9/2009). Instead, the Americans understood that sheikhs maintained their power by being able to provide resources for their tribesmen. Providing contracts would sustain the patronage system the tribes' sheikhs relied on.[2] Another tactic followed in the strategy to build the strength of the tribal system was encouraging sheikhs in exile to return to al Anbar (McCary, 2009). General Allen was particularly active in this area, spending "long hours negotiating with them, convincing the sheikhs that he would be able to provide them with power and money upon their return, in addition to their own security forces" (McCary, 2009: 50).

The American strategy also emphasized making the populace secure. Therefore, training of the Iraqi Security Forces, the army and the police, was central in their plan. The police were particularly important. Recruits would receive police training in Amman, Jordan, but they also had to be trained to fight in a paramilitary style for urban engagements. This training was done by the Americans in Camp Ramadi (MacFarland, Marine interview, 2009).The COPs were eventually turned over to Iraqi police control. The goal was to have the populace see that things were getting back to normal. Consequently, they eventually changed the "combat outposts" to "security stations" and told the people that they were building police stations (Lt. Col. William Jurney, Marine interview, 2009).

Despite the promising strategic gain, the Awakening was not happily accepted by all parties on the American side. General MacFarland noted that there were problems in getting the collaboration between the US forces and the tribes accepted elsewhere in the US military. Some officers outside of the brigade in Marine headquarters worried that this effort would result in tribal militias that would eventually fight against the central government (Smith & MacFarland, 2008; Michaels, 2010). This was the reason that the Iraqi police recruits were not permitted to guard their own neighborhoods, a practice that

MacFarland reversed (McCary, 2009). The government in Baghdad was also concerned that the Awakening would produce militias that would eventually fight against it. In addition, the Awakening leaders made no secret of their dislike of the Governor of al Anbar and asked for him to be removed, which also looked like a challenge to the central government.

General MacFarland described the Sunni tribal position and the American efforts to satisfy competing demands from the tribes for security and the demands from the central government that al Anbar would not develop sufficient forces to challenge Baghdad militarily:

> [The tribal leaders would say] "We want to defend ourselves. We don't trust the Iraqi Army to do that for us because the Iraqi Army was overwhelmingly Shi'a." Now they had a lot of Sunni officers, and they weren't fighting the Iraqi Army, they just didn't know that the central government would keep them out there to fight against Muqtada al Sadr, because they saw the Iraqi Army units look the other way in southern Iraq. So they said, "we have to have our own ability to defend ourselves." And I said ok but it can't just be tribal militia. You guys have to be integrated into the Iraqi security forces. So if they do take the 7th Iraqi Army Division of the 1st Iraqi Army division out of al Anbar you have the ability to maintain security with a non-deployable force like the police. So that was what was so attractive to them about the police and I said you know the difference between a policeman and a tribal militia guy is if he's a police man I can support him. If he's tribal militia I don't know. . . . I don't know who he is, but if I know who he is and I issue him a weapon I know the serial number, I'm going to provide you with the ammunition, the training , the material support with the logistics, you know, whatever you need with force protection measures to make him a success. This was incredibly attractive to them. This was a heavily Sunni area so to me it seemed that the best way forward was what I had seen in Bosnia when I was there as part of the Implementation force in January of '96 is separate the combatants and then you start bringing them back together again, talking over the fence about common interests and then you slowly. . . . But right now it was too mixed up for them to really deal with it. So for me the sales pitch was we'll give you a stay at home security force so whatever the central government does, you'll still have security. And the fact that they were integrated into the Iraqi security force meant that we weren't building them up as a force that the Iraqi Army or anybody else would see as a threat either. The central government had to see them as value added. (MacFarland interview 11/3/2009)

Another problem 1MEF had with Sattar was that they were trying to get the top sheikhs who had left al Anbar for safety in Jordan of Syria to come home. First, there was some concern about the central role of Sheikh Sattar. He was known to be a minor sheikh, and a smuggler, if not a murderer. By the time the Awakening began to achieve successes, the sheikhs had begun to squabble, some more important sheikhs claiming that Sattar had "stolen" their idea of an awakening. There was a conflict of constituent issue between the Army brigade working with the Awakening and 1MEF Marines trying to get the traditional top sheikhs back to al Anbar. They were concerned that an alliance with Sattar would offend the high-ranking sheikhs they were trying to convince to return to al Anbar (Micheals, 2010). One interviewee told a story that reflects this conflict. General Petraeus visited al Anbar and, after being briefed about the progress there because of the Awakening, said:

> "Why haven't I heard about this before? I've been going all around Iraq and it's crap everywhere . . . like . . . this is the best thing going on in Iraq! Why haven't I heard about this?" so, he turns over to General Gaskin, who was just new, and I think [General] Zilmer was there, and I think Allen was there, and I'm pretty sure Allen would have been there if Petraeus was there, and General Gaskin says "Sir, these are small fish. We're going after the big fish" I mean, this is right in the room where the politics are going on, where . . . they have to support the provincial council, they've got the big sheikhs that believe that this is their idea that Sattar stole, and implemented in Ramadi, and he's a nothing . . . he's a thief, you know, he steals not only things on the highway but he also steals our ideas and he's trying to take credit for it. And here's the brigade thinking . . . well, I don't care who he is, he brought us 5 thousand policemen! (This interviewee remains anonymous)

That same interviewee argued that the Marines were opposed to the efforts MacFarland and others were making, but General Allen strongly disagreed with that interpretation of events. Allen insisted that the 1MEF leadership was very supportive of MacFarland's efforts (Marine interview, 2009: 229).

The Awakening movement expanded quickly from this point. More tribes either supported or were neutral toward the Americans in the Ramadi area (Deane, 2010). As the fall of 2006 progressed, more Iraqis joined the police and army. By November, 2006, close to 3,000 men were either in the police, undergoing training, or waiting for training to begin (Deane, 2010: 86). Others not eligible for the police continued to fight AQI as militias, and eventually the Iraqi government authorized Emergency Response Units, which were essentially militias. Emergency Response Units were militias of 20 to 100 men, largely untrained, whose mission was to drive AQI out of their tribal areas (West, 2008). Four hundred new recruits joined the police in November, 2006, 1,000 joined in December, and 800 in January 2007 (Kagan, 2007: 8). By the end of October, 2006, Iraqi and US forces established a police station in central Ramadi, bringing the total number of stations to eight (Kagan, 2007: 7). It was also significant, in that it made it possible for the provincial government to actually go to work in the center of the city. In addition to recruits and a more functional provincial government, the Iraqis began to pass along intelligence to the Americans. At times this intelligence would be false, and designed to cause grief to a particular individual due to some feud, but much of it was credible.

By the end of October, most of the tribes in the northern and western areas around Ramadi had pledged allegiance to the Awakening (Smith & MacFarland, 2008). The Sufia and Julaybah areas of Ramadi were on the eastern outskirts of the city, and were AQI strongholds. The Albu Soda tribe, which occupies this area, had been neutral toward the Awakening. Sheikh Jassim of the Albu Soda tribe stated that after one of his brothers and three tribesmen were kidnapped on September 28, 2006, he openly opposed AQI, and he set up check points in the tribe's territory (Marine Interview, 2009 V.2 : 66). He went to Sheikhs Sattar and Hamid al Hais to get their assistance, often crossing the Euphrates on skiffs, or even swimming, at night to get to Sattar's compound (Michaels, 2010). He also asked for support from MacFarland's brigade, but Lieutenant Colonel James Lechner, MacFarland's deputy, told him that the brigade was not ready to offer full support yet, since he had only 17 fighters in his militia (Michaeles, 2010; Sheikh Jassim Marine interview 2009). The sheikh did have permission from Sattar, al Hais, and Lechner to man the check points, which was important when his men manning the checkpoints on November 20, 2006, were arrested. When AQI learned that this sheikh was about to join the Awakening, they initially offered him a bribe, and then attacked on November 25, 2006. Sheikh Jassim and Sheikh Abdul Rahman al-Janabi of the Albu Mahal tribe, who worked closely with Sheikh Jassim before and after the battle for Sufia, reported that AQI had 850 men in the attack (Marine Interview, 2009). Lieutenant Colonel Chuck Ferry and his unit, the First Battalion, Ninth Infantry, and the Iraqi Army moved quickly to help the Albu Sodas. As the AQI fighters fled, they were observed dragging bodies behind one of their vehicles, but their effort to terrorize the Albu Sodas again backfired, as more tribes joined the Awakening. "Within two months, every tribe in Sufia and Julaybah had declared support for the Awakening, and four new combat outposts had been constructed to secure the populations" (Smith & MacFarland, 2008: 50). Sheikhs Jassim and Abdul Rahman both noted that they began extensive "education" efforts to convince people that AQI were terrorists and to get other tribes the join the effort to rid the area of AQI for the three months after the Sufia battle, and that they were very effective (Marine Interview, 2009: 73–75).

MacFarland used the Albu Soda case as a good example of the inability to be neutral, and the desire to be part of the strongest tribe. The Albu Soda wanted to stay neutral, but AQI would not let them be neutral. When AQI attacked them, they joined the strongest tribe, the Awakening and its alliance with the United States. The competition between the tribes did not disappear once they were on the same side, and MacFarland described the importance of refereeing some of those disputes. They did this in part by starting the reconstruction of Ramadi process before the fighting was over. Clear, hold, and build actually occurred simultaneously:

> Because we owned the Jazeera area and western Ramadi, we called together a reconstruction conference. We brought all the sheikhs in . . . and we said OK, you tell us what you need. First we'll tell you what we can do for you. You tell us what you need. We'll break up into small work groups and each battalion commander had a group of sheiks from his area and then we'd say who in your area is an engineer, who owns a construction company, who is a doctor who can run a clinic, who is a teacher who can run a school and all this kind of stuff. Ok, we got it, farmers, markets, ok. So they would develop their own reconstruction plan and then that battalion commander would administer it. So the first reconstruction conference was all about we'll tell you what we can do for you and you think about what you want to do in the next reconstruction conference. They came back and said here is our plan, this is what we want, and these are the people we want to do it. We'd put resources in their pockets and then they could go back to their people and say look what I've done for you. The fight's over and good things are happening. For a while that tamped down a lot of the rivalries. (MacFarland interview, 11/3/2009)

While MacFarland's brigade made significant progress working with the sheikhs, and also rapidly increased the size of the police, Ramadi remained very violent. MacFarland's brigade was replaced by the 1st Brigade Combat Team, 3rd Infantry Division in January, 2007, under the command of Colonel John Charlton.[3] Colonel Charlton described the Ramadi he encountered as follows:

> And we drove around the town a little bit and my initial impressions were that this reminds me of a war scene, out of a WWII documentary, it was that level of damage. And this is my 3rd tour in Iraq so it wasn't like I was not used to damage and fighting and all of that. I was very familiar with Iraq. But this was a really concentrated level of damage, battle damage in that city. There were entire sections of the city that were completely destroyed, the center part of the city right across from the government center was completely destroyed. What had happened over the years was that AQ and Sunni insurgents would sit across the street in buildings across the street from the government center and fire at the government center, at the governor's office, at the provincial station was just right next to. So this was just an ongoing gun battle across Main St. Ramadi. And it got so bad that, and the buildings were near collapse, that Colonel MacFarland had ordered his engineers to just destroy that section, just rubble it so that the insurgents couldn't use it as a platform to fire on to the government center. So there is literally a five block pile of rubble in the middle of the city. Every single building . . . every one of them had at least minor battle damage, most of them were near collapse. Big huge holes in them from where bombs had been dropped or tanks had fired their main guns. It was just incredible.

> The streets, most of the streets had standing sewage and water in them, because the enemy would put these improvised explosive devices (IED) out there and every time one of those went off it would rupture a sewer or water line, which would compound the problem because if you wanted to go down that street you are wondering how many IED's are underneath that six inches of water or sewage. So it was a pretty frightening proposition to go anywhere in the town. So those were the conditions that we took over under. (Interview 12/8/2009)

Colonel Charlton estimated that they experienced 35 to 40 attacks in various forms every day. He lost ten soldiers and Marines in the first month of his tour. MacFarland introduced his successor to the sheikhs, and Charlton knew he had to advance the Awakening cooperation. He also wanted to exploit the kinetic successes of MacFarland's brigade, and on February 18, 2007, ordered a six-week campaign to clear Ramadi of AQI street by street (Interview 12/8/2009). They started in the east/southeastern part of the city because it was where the enemy was strongest. There was no American or Iraqi Army presence there. As action in this section of the city wound down, they turned to the north-central part. This area had a COP that was under constant attack. Charlton recalled that he had to ask for reinforcements because the fighting was ongoing 24 hours every day. Once they had defeated AQI there, Charlton said, "we established a large police station from what we called a joint security station right in the middle of that neighborhood and then . . . we shifted to the next part because I didn't want the enemy to reposition and catch their breath." He also wanted to send a message to the people living there that the police would remain here and provide security for them. The last part of the city to clear was the south-central part. Charlton estimated that by the end of the six-week campaign they had established a dozen new police stations with the goal of maintaining the physical and psychological separation of the people from the insurgents. He recalled that by the end of the six weeks, on March 31, "there wasn't a single shot fired in the city of Ramadi. Not one shot."

On the diplomatic side, a first goal was to push the Awakening eastward. Of particular concern was the Albu Fahad tribe, which opposed AQI, but was not entirely certain about the Awakening movement. Charlton went with Sheikh Sattar to meet with the sheikhs of the Albu Fahad and other eastern tribes. He described the meeting as follows:

> And I'm a little concerned because again there's this kind of a friction between the east and the western tribes and a lot of, from what I'm hearing from the eastern side is that it's going to be tough getting these guy together, that this is going to be an uphill battle and I'm going to have to play mediator in all this so I'm kind of expecting this to be a not so great gathering. So I get there and it's like Sattar is a rock star. All of these guys are coming up to him and kissing

> him and hugging him and it's just this atmosphere of joyous celebration. It's bizarre, the impact he has on these people, so they're having this meeting and they're reciting the poetry you know that's a typical customary thing, and I'm just amazed. Guy from a small tribe, but his clout, because he stood up to AQ, he had suffered personally members of his family had been killed. But he demonstrated that Anbar rugged individual that was very much admired in that tribal society, I think for his main attributes. (interview 12/8/2009)

Because of Sattar's influence, Charlton was able to negotiate one on one with the eastern tribes. Before long there was only one tribe in the south that they continued to have problems with. All of the others had joined with the Awakening.

Another diplomatic movement inspired by Sattar was opening lines of communication with the Imams. The Americans began to engage senior Sunni religious leaders, and discovered that they were very opposed to the extremists. Charlton ordered his subordinates to form relationships with religious leaders. They even participated in Ramadan and helped restore damaged mosques. Sermons in the mosques, an important barometer of the political atmosphere, began to reflect a new view of the Americans. According to Charlton, "Occasionally they would even say, not necessarily good things about us, but cooperate with the Americans and with the ISF because they are trying to help our neighborhoods." This produced tangible results. The Americans knew AQI would try to come back, and that they would do it subtly, often targeting a neighborhood, getting rid of moderate Imams, and replacing them with one spewing negative diatribes about the Americans. There was nothing that the Americans could do about this, but since they developed good relationships with other imams, they could ask them to intercede. According to Charlton:

> They were like a smart bomb, they just went in there and it was absolutely amazing, first they would do an evaluation of who is this guy, to determine is he really from this neighborhood, is he being intimidated and coerced? Or is he from out of town? And they would censor them on one case, they did that, or just counsel them and reprimand them, in one case they even removed a guy, they said he was from out of town and the kicked him out, literally rode him out of town on a rail. Because they had the authority to do that kind of thing. (Interview 12/8/2009)

Another area in which Sattar contributed to the American effort was in recruitment into the Iraqi Army. While they had had ample police recruits, and those recruits were turning into a professional and respected police force, recruitment into the Iraqi Army was not as robust. There were two Army brigades working with the Americans in al Anbar, but they were 50% undermanned

(Charlton interview 12/8/2009). They were also primarily Shi'a, since the Shi'a were the numerical majority in Iraq. Sattar explained that the sheikhs were not encouraging their tribal sons to join the Army because they could get shipped out to other parts of Iraq and they will be killed by the Shi'a (Charlton interview 12/8/2009). This was solved when General Patreaus went to the Minister of Defense and asked him to ensure that the Army recruits from al Anbar stayed in al Anbar for at least two years. The Americans held an Army recruitment forum two days after Sattar learned of the agreement. Five hundred potential recruits showed up, overwhelming the processors (Charlton interview 12/8/2009). The two brigades got to full strength, and were 50/50 Shi'a and Sunni.

Another important development in the spring of 2007 was a high-level recognition of the importance of the Sahawa in al Anbar. As in the MacFarland era, the Marines continued to interact with the principal sheikhs in exile in Jordan and Syria, trying to convince them to return to Iraq. As Colonel Charlton recalled, "my high headquarters was kind of looking to Amman and this group and I'm looking seeing what's happening at a lower level but watching this thing spread" (interview, 12/8/2009). However, General Allen, who had a reputation for working well with the sheikhs in exile, also recognized the importance of the grassroots Awakening, and soon General Petraeus did as well. Within months, Sheikh Sattar was seated next to President Bush at a dinner with other sheikhs and the governor of al Anbar, a reflection of the extent to which his prestige far surpassed his status as a low-ranked sheikh of a low-ranked tribe (General Allen, interview).

Sheikh Sattar was active outside of Ramadi, pushing the Awakening further among the Sunni tribes. On September 13, 2007, a few days after meeting President Bush, Sattar took the SUV given to him by Bush, to visit his horses, whose stables were on his property but outside of the secured part of his compound. As he drove back to his compound, an IED exploded. AQI had gotten to a cousin of the brother of his closest body guard, and it was an inside job. The culprits were caught. AQI gambled that Sattar's death would destroy the Awakening, but the opposite happened. His brother Ahmed was elected the head of the Awakening, and after the requisite forty days of mourning after his death the tribes held a huge parade in his honor and in defiance of AQI (Charlton interview 12/8/2009). Although there was some competition for position, and the Awakening never found an equally charismatic and effective leader after his death, the Awakening went on. It was another strategic miscalculation on the part of AQI.

In 2007 the Awakening reached the Fallujah area. AQI resisted its spread, and resorted to chemical weapons in March, 2007. They used chlorine bombs in Ramadi, Fallujah, and Amiriya. On March 16, 2007, they exploded a truck filled with explosives and chlorine gas in Albu Aifan, the village of Sheikh

Aifan of the Albu Issa tribe, in an attempt to kill several sheikhs and terrorize the population. Three children and the sheikh's mother were killed. This attack was pivotal in accelerating resistance to AQI in the Fallujah area (Ardolino, 2013a). The Awakening spread to North Babil in the spring of 2007 as well (Whiteside, personal communication).

Colonel Richard Simcock was the commander of Regimental Contact Team 6, in Area of Operation Raleigh, which included Fallujah and the surrounding areas, Amiriya and Ferris in the southwest, Zaidon in the east, Karma in the northeast, and Saqlawiyah in the northwest. Fallujah had been a hotbed of insurgent activity, but the insurgents were wounded, and by 2006 Fallujah city was under the partial control of Iraqi and US forces. Major Todd Sermarini, the senior police advisor, told author Bing West that they "own only half the city. The police react to an intell tip with fifty to a hundred cops, but they won't patrol in small teams" (2008: 259). The populace was reluctant to provide information on AQI because AQI monitored the police stations, and because they did not know the individual police officers. Based on the successes in Ramadi, the Americans, along with the Iraqi Police and Army, developed a plan called Operation Alljah to further pacify the city (Green, 2010). The operation went into effect on May 29, 2007. As in the Ramadi approach, American marines and Iraqi Police and Army forces would go in to clear an area of AQI, and this was quickly followed by a hold and build approach, restoring services, cleaning up trash, making sure people had food, etc. A central component of the operation was to get the Iraqi Police out on the streets again. They were key targets of AQI, and needed to be encouraged and trained to provide security for the city's populace. The police also came under much improved leadership with Colonel Faisal Ismael Hussein. Once a neighborhood was cleaned of AQI, the plan was to establish a police precinct with 20 to 30 officers and a police chief (Green, 2010). They were reinforced by 200–250 men who were paid to join a neighborhood watch, providing the police with information and making it more difficult for insurgents to return (Green, 2010). The districts of the city were barricaded, and a partial ban was imposed on vehicles entering the city. Personal vehicles were forbidden, only commercial vehicles and buses could enter. This was done to prevent insurgents from sneaking back into the neighborhoods, and to put a stop to car bombing.

The overall plan also involved improving security so that the mayor and city council could function. A new mayor, Mayor Saad, was brought in by local leaders and he had a reputation for honesty. He was a former member of the Republican Guard and the Americans had little history with him. They eventually formed a cooperative relationship (Green, 2010). The city council was also revived. It had not functioned well, in part because four council members had been killed in the previous year. The city council members' concern about their security increased once more when the new chairman was assassinated, followed by another one soon after. The security issue was resolved when the Americans and the Iraqi Police agreed to let family members serve as security guards and give them arms (Green, 2010).

The countryside surrounding Fallujah is very tribal. The dominant tribes were the "Zuba's in Zaidon, the Albu Issa in Amiriya, and Ferris, the Jumali in Karman and the Mohemdi in Saqlawiyah" (Roggio, 2007: 2). The Halabsa, Karabah, and Alwani tribes are also important. Violence in the countryside, the tribal lands and smaller villages, was even more severe than in the city of Fallujah. Colonel Simcock worked to increase cooperation among the tribes and the Americans in all four sectors (Roggio, 2007). The American Marines worked with the Iraqi Army and provisional security forces authorized by the Iraqi government to fight AQI.

They started in Zaidon, and worked counterclockwise with Awakening forces through Amiriya (Roggio, 2007). The Zoba' tribe in Zaidon had supported the 1920s Brigade and many became insurgents after the American invasion (West, 2008). This is the dominant tribe in Zaidon, and it was more conservative than other tribes. The central person in the Zoba's rejection of AQI was Abu Maruf, whose brother was the chief of police in Fallujah. He led his former insurgents against AQI but did not become affiliated with the Sahawa (Long, 2008).

The Albu Issa tribe began to take action against AQI early on. One sheikh (who requested anonymity) stated that they began to fight against AQI in the Amiriya area southeast of Fallujah before the Awakening. The paramount sheikh at the time was Sheikh Khamis, who was elderly and less active, and was hesitant about joining the Americans in resisting AQI (Ardolino, 2013b). Many of the tribe's members initially supported the insurgency and the tribe split into warring factions (Long, 2009; Ardolino, 2013b). Sheikh Aifan Sadun al Issawi of the Albu Issa tribe, who was the nephew of the paramount sheikh, Sheikh Khamis, was an early opponent of AQI, although his initial experiences with the US forces resulted in serious injury. He went to Jordan for four months of treatment, and after his return to Iraq, he was arrested along with two of his brothers and imprisoned in Abu Ghraib for nine months. After being released from Abu Ghraib, he was placed under house arrest. His relationship with US forces improved after they compensated him for his injuries. This made him a target of AQI. Sheikh Aifan states that he started fighting AQI openly in 2005 during the darkest years of AQI violence. He fled to Amman that same year. The paramount sheikhs of the Albu Issa tribes, Sheikh Khamis and Sheikh Kalid, both refused to fight AQI and went into exile in Amman as well. In 2006, Marine General David Reist attempted to convince Sheikh Aifan to return to Iraq (Marine interview 2009) as well as the paramount sheikh, Sheikh Khamis (Ardolino, 2013b). Sheikh Aifan stated that Sheikh Sattar reached out to him at that time suggesting they cooperate in a fight against AQI. Sheikh Aifan made a deal with the Americans to let him keep his weapons, and he returned to Iraq and started to fight AQI (Marine interview 2009: 93).

Sheik Aifan met with the Marines in the village of Zuwiyah for the first time. The Marines had doubts about his authority, since he was fairly low in the hierarchy, being the fifteenth son of the first son of the family patriarch. Many uncles and older brothers superseded him in the hierarchy (Ardolino, 2013b). The Marines met with him again on December 26, January 1, and January 6 in order to further the potentially cooperative relationship and to test his knowledge of the names and locations of insurgents. The January 6 meeting was attended by Sheikh Khamis and a Marine intelligence expert, retired CWO-5 James Roussell. Roussell played a role similar to that played by Captain Patriquin in Ramadi. Although he was not a linguist, he was an expert in counterinsurgency and a careful student of tribal and sheikh behavior (Ardolino, 2013b). He was able to identify a pattern of meetings being held among the real sheikhs of Fallujah. The Marines concluded that Sheikh Aifan did have the requisite knowledge, but they also noted that Sheikh Khamis remained aloof and noncommittal during the meeting (Ardolino, 2013b).

Sheikh Aifan made his needs clear. He wanted equipment such as cars and radios, he wanted his tribesmen in custody released, and he wanted weapons and permission for his men to carry them. He also wanted contracts like those awarded to sheikhs in the Ramadi area in order to give his tribe work. The Marines had permission to ask him for the names of thirty tribesmen who could be armed and permitted to carry weapons openly, and they also gave others permission to carry rifles close to their homes (like on rooftops) for self-defense (Ardolino, 2013b). The agreement produced a militia for the sheikh and a flood of intelligence for the marines.

Contacts were made with other sheikhs in the Albu Issa tribe. As in Ramadi, contracts were also awarded to enable the sheikhs to provide income for their tribesmen. And also as in Ramadi, there was intense competition among the sheikhs for American contracts. The Americans awarded contracts in particular to those sheikhs they wanted to empower, those who were close to paramount Shiekh Khamis, those who provided the best intelligence, and those militias who worked aggressively against AQI (Ardolino, 2013b).

The paramount sheikh of the Jumaly tribe in Karma was Sheikh Mishan. In our interview with him, he stated that he initially supported and defended the Americans, for which he was condemned (interview 2/6/2010). He fled Fallujah in 2005 after hearing reports that he had been killed and later received a phone call asking him, as the sheikh, to resolve a dispute. This, he suspected, was a set up so he said he was in Baghdad and could not come. He went to Syria. Within a month, one of his sons was kidnapped and beheaded

(Interview, 3/6/2010). Sheikh Mishan stayed in Syria until early 2006, when he got a call asking him to come to Amman where he met with General Allen, who asked him to return to Fallujah. He told Allen he would not go back, that the Americans had taken their weapons and left them defenseless to face "opals [which would] come with foreigners with weapons, masks, who come and take leaders of tribes. A son can't defend his father. Americans watch and do nothing" (Interview 3/6/2010). When General Allen said they would protect him, the sheikh said he did not trust him.

Sheikh Mishan lost another son in 2007 to a roadside IED. The son was attempting to deliver money to tribal members in Karma. Three days after that son's funeral Sheikh Mishan returned to Karma to lead the fight against AQI. He gathered his tribal members and told them they should all go back. The sheikh also had them swear on the Holy Koran that all feuds would cease, and there would be no revenge taking. He was assisted in his efforts by Brigadier General John Allen who provided transportation on a C130, and arranged for the training and equipping of a 1,000-man Provincial Security Force (West, 2008).

Although Shiekh Mishan's cousin, Major General Sadun Talib al-Jumayli, led the local resistance to AQI and joined the Sahawa, once Mishan returned, the cousin accepted Mishan's leadership (Long, 2008). Mishan claims that all of the tribes within a 20-kilometer range joined the Awakening. He also complained about being held back by the Americans for a few days before being able to move ahead and drive AQI back. AQI did not go willingly (interview 3/6/2010). AQI bombed three of his family members' houses, and then bombed a fourth house with ten family members inside (Totten, 2008). Sheikh Mishan recalled one attack from the north by terrorists who were fully armed, had trucks loaded with TNT, and who planned to destroy all the buildings on the main road (Interview 3/6/2010). Sheikh Mishan also stated that ten days after combat began, the person who killed his son with the IED was captured and brought to him. He remembered his oath not to seek revenge, and forgave the murderer, who said AQI forced him to plant the IED.

After AQI was on the run, they formed a tribal council with Mishan as the head. They met every Thursday. On June 26, 2008, the sheikh missed the meeting, and told us that the reason was a very bad headache (Interview, 3/6/2010). A suicide bomber attacked the meeting, killing 26 Iraqis, including Mishan's brother, uncle (interview, 3/6/2010), the mayor of Karma, and three Marines, among whom was a Marine battalion commander (Long, 2008). Major General Sadun al-Jumayli stated that Sheikh Mishan had "interfered in security arrangements" for the meeting, which is how the attack happened (Dagher, 2009). In any case, Sheikh Mishan was pushed out of the tribal council and the leadership reverted back to Major General Sadun. When we interviewed Mishan in 2010, he had returned to Amman.

Gradually, the Awakening spread to additional provinces in Iraq, including Ninewah, Salah al Din, Kirkuk, North Babil, and Diyala Provinces (Dale, 2009). Violence by AQI continued, but al Anbar became a relatively peaceful province in Iraq as a consequence of the Awakening. Later, the tribes had returned to normal competition. The Iraq Body Count (https://www.iraqbodycount.org/database/) documentation of civilian deaths graphically shows the decline in violence by 2008.

The data show the dramatic impact of the Awakening on violence in al Anbar from its beginning to 2008, at which point it spread across the province. Also by 2008, over 11,000 AQI members had been killed or captured and foreign fighters arriving in Iraq to fight for AQI began to dwindle. By 2009, only five or six entered Iraq per month, down from 120 in 2007 (Kirdar, 2011: 5). Ironically, the decrease in foreign fighters helped ISIS in the reemergence of violence, which will be discussed in the Epilogue.

Table 5.1 Civilian Deaths Caused by Insurgents

2004	*2005*	*2006*	*2007*	*2008*
238	439	435	521	177

Table 5.2 Civilian Deaths by All Combatants

2004	*2005*	*2006*	*2007*	*2008*
2,247	1,182	1,458	1,951	589

CONCLUSION

In summary, after the Awakening took hold in Ramadi, it spread quickly from city to city. Ramadi's Awakening was particularly important for at least three reasons: First, it was the provincial capital and its liberation from AQI eventually allowed the provincial government to function; second, it was the site of a formal organization for the Sahawa; and third, it demonstrated the resources the Americans were willing and able to bring to the area to help rebuild after the destruction of war. Confidence building by the Americans was very important. The Sheikhs communicated regularly about what was happening, military strategy, and intelligence. With each successful action against AQI came increased security, more police, and the presence of the Iraqi Army.

After the successes by the Awakening movement and the defeat of AQI, reports of infighting in the Awakening movement itself emerged. While there was always suspicion among some sheikhs about the Awakening as an organization, some sheikhs began to worry that the Awakening organization would become a political vehicle that would threaten the authority of tribal sheiks. Ahmed Albu Risha demonstrated early signs of wanting to use the Awakening organizations for his own political advantages. He opened offices in Karma, in the Jumayli tribal area, and was allegedly disrespectful to Sheikh Mishan when the sheikh accused Albu Risha of stirring up trouble (Interview 3/6/2010).

As time passed there were growing divisions among the tribal sheikhs in the Awakening movement and it became increasingly politicized. Hamid al Hais was expelled from the Sahawa organization by Sattar, and formed his own awakening organization, the National Front for the Salvation of Iraq. In February 2008, al Hais and Ali Hatim accused the IIP of unfair influence in official posts and gave them 30 days to get out of the province (Ali, 2008). He also suggested that the IIP was in league with AQI. Ahmed Albu Risha criticized al Hais and Hatim for this and formed an alliance with the IIP. In June, 2008, Albu Risha and al Hais formed a joint organization, called (again) The Anbar Salvation Council, which was to be a political vehicle for the 2009 provincial elections. This alliance did not last long, and by December, 2008, Ahmed Albu Risha formed an alliance with the National Gathering of Independents, which was linked to the IIP, and he did not consult other Awakening Council members about this (Niquash, 2009). This caused forty of the Awakening Council members to walk out and join al Hais and Ali Hatim in the Iraq's Tribes List (Wing, 2008).

By the time the 2010 national parliamentary elections approached, the three former Awakening allies had changed again. Albu Risha allied the Awakening Council with the Iraq's Unity coalition, which included the Iraqi Constitutional Party, led by Interior Minister Jawad al-Bolani (Carnegie Endowment for International Peace, 2010). Al Hais ran on an Anbar Salvation Council ticket, which is considered "Iranian" because al Hais went to Iran in 2009, and because of its alliance with the Iraq National Alliance coalition. This coalition includes Islamist Shi'a such as Moqtada al Sadr (Carnegie Endowment, 2010). Ali Hatim founded the Anbar Salvation National Front and announced an alliance with a Shi'a politician from Karbala named Yousef al Habboubi. Together they announced the formation of an alliance called Banners of Iraq (Niquash, 2009).

The politicization of the Awakening movement was condemned by a number of our Iraqi interviewees. Sheikh Majed, for example, believes that the Americans politicized the tribes, they were never political before. Sheikh Tariq, on the other hand, noted that Sheikhs who were educated have always participated in parliament, but to have a party is unusual (3/10/2010). Sheikh Sabbah stated that "the Sahawah in the Ramadi area has become a political party and I think this is the beginning of the end. When they have become a political party. I think they will get one or 2 seats in this election [March 2010]. Because they are not politicians. Politics involve always lying and sheikhs cannot do that. Once they begin lying and playing games they lose the respect of the people and their authority" (Interview 3/10/2010).

NOTES

1. The term Anbar Salvation Council evokes a great deal of confusion. Aakab al Gaood believes it was his father Faisal's creation and the foundation of the Awakening in Anbar. Ahmed Albu Risha's official response to our questions states that it was created in 2006 for the sole purpose of negotiating with the Maliki government and should then have been dissolved. This hints about the dissatisfaction many members of the Awakening felt toward Hamid al Hais by 2009 when he revitalized the term as his own political vehicle for the 2010 elections. It is regarded by some of the original Awakening leadership to be Iranian, because al Hais has gone to Iran and is now regarded with great suspicion.
2. This is why the military did not follow the usual American practice of requiring competitive bids, awarding the contract to the lowest bidder (McCary, 2009).
3. Go Cougs!

Chapter 6

Epilogue and Conclusions

In the time since the interviews of Sunni tribal leaders presented here, the situation in al Anbar has changed considerably. In this chapter we will examine some of the developments since 2010 in light of the factors we used to explain the Awakening. Many of the security gains and political cooperation achieved through the Awakening and US collaboration have been lost. The general security situation has declined significantly and, while AQI struggled for several years after the Awakening, it recovered its strength, taking advantage of the chaos in Syria, and evolved into the Islamic State of Iraq and al-Sham (ISIS). ISIS is no longer in alliance with AQ Central, a split that was likely inevitable given the transitions in leadership in both organizations. In the midst of increased physical insecurity, there also developed deepening political divides between Sunni and Shiite political groups. All of this indicates that Iraqi society has increasingly fractured along the identity fault lines identified in this book. The threat perceptions, assumptions and suspicions of motivations, and characteristics of the various groups identified in this study all appear to have increased, or at least to be operating in an environment of increased political turmoil and political violence. Various political maneuvering reflecting the deep-seated distrust and suspicions between the Sunni and Shiite groups in Iraq continued to be the central political dilemma in governing the nation of Iraq.

The Sunni population in al Anbar find themselves in a position not unlike their previous predicament of feeling marginalized and apart from the political process in Baghdad, which combined with the perceived persecution of the American forces led them to their initial, albeit brief, alliance with AQI and has contributed to some support of ISIS more recently. As discussed in previous sections of this book, this period of alienation led to violent conflict with Baghdad, US forces, and eventually to the shift in allegiances by the

Sunni tribes. The period of cooperation with the central government of Baghdad presented an opportunity for trust building and a pathway to integrating al Anbar and Sunni identities into a superordinate Iraqi identity as they fought a common enemy in AQI in defense of their tribes and the Iraqi nation.

However, this window of opportunity, in the years since, has been dramatically slammed shut by political events in Iraq, and most dramatically in the more recent months as ISIS has grown in strength. The central government in Baghdad, led by the coalition government of al-Maliki, has made a series of decisions that have served to confirm and consolidate the threatening image of the Shiite government held by the Sunni tribes. The following section addresses the general political and security environment in al Anbar after 2014. Events are shifting so rapidly that no attempt to review them can be current.

The political fractures in Iraq appear to be based on many of the same divisions that existed before and during the Awakening movement, as Sheikh Humaid al-Dulaimi has stated, "The splits witnessed in Anbar since the eruption of anti-government protests on Dec. 23, 2012, the developments that came after the formation of the government-backed Sahawa organizations, led by Sheikh Wissam al Hardan—notably that former Sahawa leaders Sheikh Ahmad abu Risha and Ali al Hatim joined the opposition—in addition to the Syrian crisis, its repercussions and the bad security management are all factors contributing" to the latest collapse in security (Abbas, 2013). Dulaimi has claimed that Sahawa leadership is now directly targeted by al-Qaeda, and engaged in a battle to "exterminate them" (Abbas, 2013).

SECURITY IN IRAQ AND AL-ANBAR

The security situation in al Anbar continues to deteriorate at a rapid pace at the time of writing. Approximately 443 people were killed by insurgents in al Anbar in 2013 (Iraq Body Count https://www.iraqbodycount.org/database), a five-year high. While this number is significantly lower than peak levels of 2007, it marks a sharp increase in violence from the previous five years. Meanwhile, death squads, militia groups, and rogue or former al-Qaeda, and ISIS militants have taken over abandoned military outposts, police stations, and even major cities in al Anbar such as Falluja and Ramadi (Abdul-Zahra, 2014), along with large metropolitan centers outside of al Anbar, such as Mosul. These events demonstrate a substantial loss of whatever political progress and cooperation made between Sunni tribes and Sunni political groups and Shiite coalition government during the Awakening. The deteriorating security situation represents a failure of a transition of the successful military cooperation between the Sunni Awakening and the central government to political cooperation. Currently, it appears ISIS and other al Qaeda-affiliated insurgents, along with former Ba'athist elements, have made substantial headway into al Anbar region in Fallujah (and the Ninewa region) once again. At the same time, we see substantial division not just between Sunni and Shiite political groups, but fractures in Sunni parties as well. And, as will be discussed in the upcoming section, the recent political crisis has resulted in a splintering in the small numbers of Sunni-Shiite nonsectarian political coalitions that do exist in Baghdad, in particular within the National Iraqiya coalition led by Ayed Allawi. This section will summarize the political and security situation in Iraq since the Awakening and use ensuing events to further understand the Sahawa movement.

MILITARY PROGRESS FOLLOWED BY POLITICAL FAILINGS

After winning a plurality of seats in the 2010 elections, the predominantly Sunni al-Iraqiya party, led by Allawi, failed to assemble a government, and in the ensuing 7 months the al-Iraqiya party was outmaneuvered by al Maliki as he formed the State of Law Coalition. Maliki then proceeded to cobble together a successful coalition and assumed power in 2011 (Habib, 2013). As a result of these events, and for the involvement of seven al-Iraqiya members in Maliki's government, Allawi was promised high-ranking positions by Maliki (Habib, 2013) in his new government. These promises were not entirely fulfilled, and in fact a series of power consolidation maneuvers and efforts at marginalizing Sunni political leaders quickly followed the formation of Maliki's government in 2011 (Habib, 2013).

Maliki's leadership was largely viewed by outside observers as divisive and exclusionary toward Sunni political groups (International Crisis Group, Morris 2014). As discussed earlier, the de-Ba'athification process played an integral role in the Sunni tribes ultimately cooperating with the insurgency and AQI. In this light, the Iraqi Parliament passed the "Law of Supreme National Commission for Accountability and Justice" in 2008, as an attempt to reform the previous de-Ba'athification laws that were so threatening to Sunni identity and greatly contributed to the sense of marginalization (Deyoung, 2014). The International Center for Transitional Justice has noted several areas in which the Justice and Accountability Law is an improvement on previous de-Ba'athification policy. Namely, these improvements include the clarification of pension rights, and levels of Ba'ath party to which dismissal would be applied (ICTJ, 2008). However, observers note that the system was largely built on a "guilt by association" construct and that de-Bathification would continue without any kind of time limit (ICTJ, 2008), and did not dissolve the previous de-Ba'athification office (ICTJ, 2008). Maliki was accused by various Sunni leaders of using the Justice and Accountability Law as a political weapon, in particular against those Sunnis who did not maintain political loyalty to his coalition. As Rafie Rifai, the Mufti of Iraq and a Sunni cleric, says, "Maliki is selective in dealing with the Accountability and Justice Law, because many employees at his office would be affected by this law. However, he is enforcing it on university professors and ordinary people." (Abel Sadah, 2013).

The trend of persecuting Sunni political leaders went beyond "ordinary people," however, as eventually Vice President Tariq al- Hashemi and Deputy Prime Minister Rafi al-Issawi faced arrest charges for accusations of al Qaeda and terrorist support (Abel Sadah, 2013). The merits of these accusations can certainly be debated; however, in the context of deep suspicion held by Sunnis and the images and perceptions detailed in this research, they acquired a certain meaning for Sunni people and political leaders. They were a reminder of the previous marginalization and persecution they felt during the Bremer/Provisional government period, as a consequence which they felt compelled to defend themselves by embarking on an insurgency and participating with AQI. The Sunnis tribal leaders have expressed a deep sense of threat from the Shiite political parties since the overthrow of Saddam Hussein, and these persecutions only evoked and built on that threat perception in the post-Sahawa environment.

The arrests of Sunni politicians by Maliki's forces provoked protests by the Sunni population (Namaa 2013). Maliki responded to these protests with accusations by claiming that the Sunnis had become "support cells" for terrorism and al-Qaeda, and ordered troops to break up the protest camps (Namaa, 2013). The incursions by Maliki's security forces into these protests led to civilian deaths and further political fractures in the already weakening relationship between the Sunni tribes and the Shiite coalition government. The Sunni cleric Sheikh Abdul Malik Al-Saddi called on the protesters to remain peaceful but denounced the security force incursion while urging Sunni ministers, local officials, and Parliament members to resign and boycott the political process entirely (Namaa, 2013).

FRACTURING OF THE IRAQIYA PARTY

In the time since (and likely because of) the failure of Allawi and the Iraqiya party to assemble a government despite winning a plurality of votes in 2010, the more nonsectarian Iraqiya party has experienced a splintering of alliances. The Iraqiya split represented a further weakening of Sunni political power, and suggests a weakening of nonsectarian political identities in Iraqi politics. The broader coalition that once made up the party split into three competing factions. The United Bloc is composed of fourteen Sunni groups and tribes and is led by Usama al-Nujaifi, the speaker of the council of representatives. The Iraqi Front for National Dialogue is led by Deputy Prime Minister Saleh al-Mutlaq. Finally, the remnants of Ayed Allawi's coalition are composed of Sunni, Shiite, and some tribal interests (Habib, 2013). This three-way splintering of Iraqiya left Nujaifi and Allawi as the prime competitors for Sunni tribal support, while al-Mutlaq was seen by many Sunnis to be too close to al-Maliki, and has been subjected to Sunni protests (Habib, 2013). The weakening of the Iraqiya party represented a significant loss of Sunni political access to Baghdad, and also illustrates how overtly nonsectarian politics began to fail in Iraq. This only heightened the sense of threat and isolation in the minds of Sunni leaders.

RESURGENT SUNNI MILITANTS AND FUNDAMENTALISTS

The reemergence of AQI-related insurgent groups and the presence of ISIS in al Anbar presented the Sunni tribes and the Awakening figures with a familiar dilemma. In the face of an increased insurgent presence, Sunni leaders were faced once again with the prospect of making allies with the fundamentalists operating in their region, or fighting them in alliance with the government (and this time, without the same kind of cooperation and participation of coalition and US ground forces). Adding to the complexity of the situation, however, was the fact that the ISIS groups may have learned from their previous failures in al Anbar and their utter failure to first infiltrate and then dismantle the tribal structure. After the initial successes of the Awakening, many AQI militants were imprisoned in Camp Bucca where they regrouped and planned for their future operations once they were released from prison (Whiteside, 2015). As the ISIS presence and conquests increased after 2010, mixed reports emerged of how the insurgent militants were dealing with local populations, tribes, and tribal leaders. In this section we will discuss some of the mixed reports of the relationship the tribes have with ISIS and AQI and discuss whether this can provide any insight into how the tribes may respond to the advances made by ISIS into cities like Fallujah and Mosul.

Some evidence suggests ISIS appeared to have a new strategy with at least some of the tribes and the Sunni population after AQI's ruinous experience in al Anbar. The recent events of Anbar offer conflicting reports of both tribal cooperation with ISIS and also a return of active tribal confrontation and violent conflict with ISIS. The issue of tribal cooperation with or military opposition to ISIS is in part related to their use of extreme forms of violence, particularly against civilians. This issue has been part of the long road to the separation of AQI with AQC, and the distain with which AQI's new manifestation as ISIS has of AQC. Even in the early years when AQI was under the leadership of Albu Musab al Zarqawi, AQC cautioned against the brutal tactics and targeting of fellow Muslims. By the time Abu Bakr al-Baghdadi took over in 2010, the distance between them was growing. By February 2014, AQC cut all ties with ISIS. ISIS claimed a merger with Jabhat al-Nusra in Syria in 2013. However, this claimed merger on the part of ISIS leader Abu Bakr al-Baghdadi is denied by both Al Qaeda Central and Jabhat al-Nusra of the Levant. However, reports also indicate that ISIS and Jabhat al-Nusra are cooperating in some areas of Syria. It is apparent that the relationship between AQ central, and ISIS and al Nusra is complex and fragmented, at best.

At the same time, there are reports indicating that tribes in Syria are combating ISIS presence in their areas, as they are viewed as predominantly outsiders. This relationship is contrasted with the apparent acceptance of Jabhat al Nusra by the tribes and other Syrian rebel factions in their ongoing civil war, because Jabhat al Nusra is viewed as both a more local presence in Syria and is reported to have a less brutal hand in dealing with competitors or rivals for power than ISIS. These reports indicate that the behaviors AQI exhibited in al Anbar that contributed to the breaking of their temporary alliance with the tribes—and their eventual perception of AQI as a barbarian actor—still persist to this day under the current insurgency against ISIS.

All of this raises an important question of whether or not the tactics of ISIS/AQI changed significantly enough to promote a change in the adversarial relationship that eventually developed between the tribes of al Anbar and AQI, leading up to the Awakening. Early on in ISIS' surge to power, some reports indicated a softer hand on the part of ISIS in Iraq, even though other reports abound of brutality and atrocities. It may be explained by some recognition on the part of ISIS of the narrative portrayed here: that their brutality toward the tribes and local population has been a major contributor to the collapse of their cooperation and the eventual Awakening movement. Reports indicated a possible changed strategy of attempts to win the "hearts and minds" of the locals through providing food and supplies at various ISIS-funded bakeries, for instance. One observer notes that ISIS strategy has been much more conciliatory then was initially expected when it moved into Fallujah recently (Pasha, 2014). Reports indicate residents of Fallujah claiming that the current fighters occupying their city are more accommodating, bringing fuel and much needed supplies to the residents of Fallujah (Ghazi & Arango, 2014).

This time, the Sunni militants and fundamentalists were no longer justifying their presence in al Anbar by fighting invading infidels as AQI was in the early stages of the US invasion. While some sources indicate they were selling themselves to the tribes as joint defense forces against Shiite political aggression and the central government, and against the "Safavid" army of Maliki (Sinjari, 2013), they actually began reformulating their strategy as early as 2006 when the Mujahideen Shura Council was formed. As noted earlier, it has been suggested that part of the reduced presence of Zarqawi was an effort to obscure the extent to which AQI leadership was not Iraqi. The ISIS Iraqi leadership that emerged after the defeat by the Awakening is Iraqi.[1] This allowed them to link identities with the Sunni Iraqis; they could maintain that they are the same people.

In addition, ISIS began to take advantage of the weakness of the Awakening as an organization. Recall that the Awakening brought together tribal leaders who normally are competitive. After their success, they began to return to their competitive ways. The Awakening did not enter politics as a block. There was in fact considerable dispute as to whether the sheikhs should engage in politics at all. As one interview participant explained:

> See the tribal leaders are not political leaders they have no idea what politics is they never did. The tribal leader is a man who looks after his tribe opens gates, and doors, and guest houses, each tribe leader has guest houses like Sheikh Majed now he's got his house open, and all trouble or any problem in their tribe, the sheikh is there to sort it out for them. They've never been interfered in politics until recently more or less. But prior to that he's just a man who's inherited to become the leader of this tribe and that's the job he farms and some people work for him and he makes money out of it and whatever contribution comes from central government or other but he's never been the political side. This is what I'm saying is the mistake as he said now with the coalition with the Awakening we brought what is known as the tribal heads become political. (Anonymous)

Given the competitiveness of the tribal system, and the fact that Ahmad Albu Risha, who was not the leader his brother Sattar was, was attempting to lead the Awakening into the political system, there were defections, expulsions, and distrust. ISIS was able to take advantage of the inherent weakness of the Awakening once the survival of the tribes was no longer in question. They began to systematically target leaders of the Awakening who maintained their allegiance to the Awakening for death. For example, Ahmed Albu Risha's nephew, Mohammed Khamis, was assassinated on June 3, 2014 in Anbar province by ISIS in a targeted killing. Mohammed Khamis Albu Risha was serving as head of the Ramadi Awakening Council at the time of his assassination (Tawfeeq & Carter, June 3 2014). Rather than targeting the entire tribal system, ISIS became able to capitalize "on divided households and clans that provided detailed information on the movements of Awakening members" (Whiteside, 2015: 2). They took advantage of the competiveness within the tribal system as well as the disruption of the social hierarchies within the tribes caused by the pre-Awakening conflict that placed low-ranking sheikhs in important positions. In addition to the pre-Awakening-style coercion, ambitious tribal members became willing to identify relatives who ISIS targeted, whom ISIS targeted. ISIS also courted tribal leaders with gifts (Whiteside, 2015). In summary, they provided a correction to two previous crucial causes of their earlier failure; the barbarian image of the insurgent held by the tribes is cracked by their identity as Iraqis, and by their use of "carrots" to induce the tribes to give them another look (Whiteside, 2015). Second, they did not pose a threat to the core identity of the tribal members, the tribal system, but to individuals in the system. Finally, ISIS has been able to take advantage of the growing disillusionment among the Sunni population after the aforementioned incursions into a protest camp spurred by Maliki's arrest of Sunni lawmakers; ISIS saw the opportunity in presenting itself to Anbar Sunnis as a defender against Maliki and Shiite political domination.

ISIS has had mixed results. It appears that some tribes or clans have joined the insurgents in their struggle against the government. Sheikh Rafai Mishhin al-Jumaili, of the Jumaili tribe, whose father was actually a leader of the Sahawa in the Karma area of Fallujah (Morris, 2014), made the case that his tribe joined ISIS as a response to the Iraqi military's aggression toward his tribe. As he explained, after having fought al-Qaeda alongside American troops, he now fights with ISIS because, "If the army moves forward to kill you, are you going to receive him with flowers? No. We are going to defend ourselves." Jumaili also accused those of fighting with the government to be traitors to the Sunni tribes and pursuing personal interests (Morris, 2014). This represents a powerful and an important shift yet again, in the complex relationship between the tribes, the insurgents, and the Shiite-led central government. It also indicates an utter loss of opportunity for capitalizing on the cooperation that once existed between the tribes and the central government.

However significant this latest shift may be to the balance of power in al Anbar, it does not appear to be universal or even widespread across the Sunni tribes. For his part, the brother of the "founder" of the Awakening movement, Ahmed Albu Risha, is fighting alongside the government against the latest advances by ISIS. However, even he provides a qualifying statement of his level of comfort in working with the Sunni-led central government: "We still obviously have our issues with the government," Albu Risha said. "But at the moment, al-Qaeda [ISIS] is the biggest problem" (Morris, 2014). Albu Risha expressed very much the same sentiment in the interviews conducted earlier in the research, "The reason why we returned to carry our weapons and fight is because Qaeda [ISIS] returned to our cities . . . we are obliged to defend ourselves and our province" (Arango & Fahim, 2014). However, Albu Risha added an important thought regarding any sense of nationalism or a superordinate identity in the struggle against ISIS. He said that the Albu Risha tribe and other Sunni tribes of the Awakening joined the struggle once again, "not to fight for Americans or the Iraqi government" (Arango & Fahim, 2014). Here we see a key figure in the Awakening movement explicitly distancing himself and the struggle from the US and the Iraqi government. Albu Risha also demonstrated that the identity of the tribe is what he and others are interested in defending. Once again, tribal identity is fundamental.

Based on journalistic accounts, Ahmed Albu-Risha's lukewarm sentiment toward a working relationship with the central government is shared by other tribal leaders. There appears to be a widespread sense of abandonment by the Iraqi government. Another figure in the Awakening movement explained, "The government called us back a month ago. . . . until now, they have given us nothing but promises—no weapons, and no money. We have depended on ourselves even to buy uniforms" (Arango & Fahim, 2014). A spokesman for a Sunni political party explained it in more stark terms, "Sunnis were stuck in the middle between al-Qaeda's hammer and Maliki's neglect" (Arango & Fahim, 2014). The accusations of lack of pay, neglect since the formation of the new coalition government, and political persecution left the Sahawa "dead" (Arango & Fahim, 2014). Despite these perceptions, Maliki and the central government were once again in the position of facing a military and political opponent, which it seemingly cannot defeat on its own and cannot protect the country's own borders from its advance. As in the past, it

> attempted to build a military alliance with the Sunni tribesman in the conflict with ISIS and Sunni insurgent fundamentalist groups. In exchange for pulling security forces out of Fallujah and Ramadi, and hinting towards amnesty for militants who may have participated in armed resistance against the government, Maliki hoped to gain, at the least, a military ally, while others in his party hoped it would be a further and renewed step towards political reconciliation. Osama al-Nujaifi voiced considerable suspicion about a possible new alliance with the government, as he explained; "From 2006 to 2008, tribesmen were able to beat al-Qaeda with the cooperation of American forces and the support of the Iraqi government. . . . After gaining victory over al-Qaeda, those tribesman were rewarded with the cutting of their salaries, with assassination and displacement." After their efforts to root out AQI, the fighters of the Awakening movement were, he says, "left in the street facing revenge from al-Qaeda and neglect by the government." (Arango & Fahim, 2014)

The Sunni tribal leaders view the Maliki government as one that has attempted to dismantle the Awakening political and military movement through marginalization, hindering the flow of resources (including pay and weapons for security forces), and targeted imprisonments. Then the Maliki government once again turned to the tribes for assistance in dealing with the

ISIS threat. The Sunni tribal leaders perceived this as an attempt by Maliki to engage the tribes out of military necessity rather than an attempt at true political accommodation to the tribes and Sunnis. As the Sunni political leader explains, "We reject our sons being rentals," Ani said. "They are used like a disposal [*sic*] tissue, to wipe up the problems and then thrown away" (Morris, 2014, Arango & Fahim, 2014).

Despite these various reports that ISIS may have changed its tactics in some ways, there is ample evidence that serious conflict exists and remains between the tribes and ISIS, and that ISIS is generally viewed as too harsh and extreme for Sunni residents (and, it appears that this goes for the Syrian tribes as well). The radical cleric Abdullah al-Janabi, who gained notoriety as a former emir in the Mujahideen Shura Council, a precursor to the Islamic State of Iraq, has once again emerged as a prominent figure in ISIS. He is known for his harsh Islamic courts and rulings that executed many for suspicion of collusion with the United States and enforced harsh rulings. Al Janabi has recently emerged as a central power figure in Fallujah, and has instituted courts and committees such as the "Committee for the Promotion of Virtue and Prevention of Vice." Further, while there are reports of ISIS-led bakeries and other social service efforts in Fallujah, there are also reports of ISIS implementing harsh and fundamentalist practices on populations—so while they may be opening bakeries in communities, they are at the same time demanding that women and men attend separate bakeries.

Changed tactics or not, it is apparent that some tribes in the Fallujah area are cooperating with ISIS in spite of the past or present experiences of brutality. And while there exists an emerging effort on the part of the tribes and Baghdad to remove ISIS from Fallujah and Ramadi, there remains this crucial element that some tribes, especially in and around Fallujah, have aligned with ISIS in response to the perception that the central government is excluding them from the political process. Iraq's deputy national security adviser, Safa Rasul Hussein, has noted that some tribes are very fractured in their allegiances, "We've seen in some tribes, the father has a position and his son has a different position. . . . Some from the tribes are fighting with ISIS, but some are also fighting against them" (Arraf, *Washington Post*, March 12 2013). The emergence of revolutionary tribal military councils in al Anbar presents a complicated picture in which tribes are sometimes launching attacks against the government forces in the area, at times in cooperation with ISIS and at other times attacking ISIS. Accounts of which tribes specifically are participating with ISIS are scarce. The Albu Nimr tribe has joined the Military Council of the Anbar Tribal Revolutionaries, and this indicates a potential hardening of defenses around Fallujah in the face of a government incursion into Fallujah. At the same time, the Muslim Scholars Association, led by Sunni clerics, has said it coordinates closely with the tribal military council for revolutionaries, and some of its officials acknowledge that they are in a temporary alliance with al Qaeda (but reports do not distinguish an alliance with ISIS). In a recent interview, Muslim Scholar Association leader Sheikh Mohammed Bashar has said the aim of the tribes fighting the government is to liberate the country from the influence of Iran (Arraf), which reinforces the interview data collected in this research that Iran is a threat manifested in the Maliki government. The familiar image of Maliki as a puppet of Iranian influence and a threat to the country remains strong among the Sheikhs. It is noteworthy in this relationship that tribes within Fallujah have at times explicitly expressed that ISIS is not in control of the city, and instead that the tribes possess the city and that the city is in conflict with the Baghdad government (Ali, ISW). Media reports from Fallujah indicate a mixed picture of popular support of Al Qaeda, whereas some reports indicate that residents "hate the government more than Al Qaeda" (Ghazi & Arango, 2014). As one Fallujah resident expressed, "We had no food, no electricity and no water, and mortar shells were falling all around us. . . . But many of us would rather support Al Qaeda than the army that has led to this massacre" (Ghazi & Arango, 2014). It appears that the tribes in the region are again threats from various sides.

REPLICATING THE AWAKENING

Immediately following the relative success of the Sahawa movement, there was much discussion, and consideration to seek tribal engagement in other areas of US operations against al Qaeda, most prominently in Afghanistan. These aspirations for "exporting" or replicating an "Awakening" in other regions of the world against al Qaeda Central (AQC), ISIS, or the Taliban and other expansion-seeking fundamentalist groups require a careful examination of structures and features of the political, geographical, economic, and tribal terrains of al Anbar in order to accurately assess the value of future efforts to emulate the Awakening. A thorough analysis of the compatibility of an Awakening movement as a policy model in various regions is beyond the scope of this present research. However, the analysis of the features in al Anbar that facilitated the initial success of the Sahawa movement is useful in considering its general applicability in other regions and in helping us better understand the particular features and conditions of the movement. Further, as Iraq is faced yet again with a strengthening and emboldened fundamentalist extremist group, it is useful to examine some of the characteristics of the region and the movement that facilitated the Sahawa's success, so that we may identify what may have changed since that period of success before assuming we can simply repeat the process.

The working, if somewhat distrustful, relationship between the tribes and the central government in Baghdad prior to the Awakening helped facilitate cooperation as the Sahawa spread through al Anbar and other provinces of Iraq. As detailed in the previous sections of this book, the tribes in al Anbar had a history of working with Baghdad in a negotiated power sharing, or at least an understanding that they could aid each other. Obviously, this history is checkered with repression and conflict; however, as noted earlier, Saddam increasingly began to rely on the tribes to help manage Iraq during the slow decline of his regime during the 1990s. The tribes in al Anbar were part of a symbiotic relationship by 2003, and were thus both invested in and accustomed to a working relationship with the political core. This relationship rewarded them with weapons, resources, and prestige and influence in their region at various points in history. By 2007, the United States and Baghdad had endorsed the wider Sahawa and it enjoyed support from more prominent sheikhs, giving it widespread support and legitimacy across the region and in the country. By 2008, the Sahawa security forces were incorporated into Iraqi security forces and were receiving funding from the central government in Baghdad—at least until around 2010 when this funding seems to have been cut off. In this way, the Sahawa was, however temporarily, a unifying force politically in the state of Iraq during the occupation and postwar reconstruction. However, it is clear that the Awakening movement presented a threat and a challenge to Baghdad, which remains problematic to this day. In this light, any proposed project of using tribes to counter a terrorism or insurgency should include careful analysis of the power relationship that tribes have with the center of economic and political power in the state. The question should be asked, and answered carefully, as to whether or not an armed tribal movement has any kind of history of successfully working with the central government, and if so, will this endorsement of a tribal militia movement strengthen or weaken that relationship.

Another prominent feature of the Awakening involves perception of AQI as an invasive foreign force not composed of leadership of the locals, The tribal members we interviewed viewed AQI as a foreign force composed of fighters from outside their own culture and nationality, and perhaps most importantly, outside their social identity group. The tribes did not see AQI as a home-grown group composed of their own, even if some of their local youths did participate in it. The research presented here illustrates the Sunni tribal leaders increasingly saw AQI as foreign occupiers who attempted to usurp political power and impose a new political and religious order upon the tribal regions of al Anbar. This perception was a key motivational drive for participation in the Sahawa for the tribes, and it is thus reasonable to assume it as a key indicator for probable success of a similar effort in another region. As mentioned, the leadership of ISIS in Iraq is Iraqi, making this element problematic for a repeat Awakening. However, there is evidence supporting this assumption currently ongoing, just across the border of al Anbar, in Syria. ISIS is facing tribal competition in parts of Syria as it is viewed as composed of foreign fighters (potentially joined with the Assad regime), whereas Jabhat Al-Nusra is finding more local support by Syrians and various Syrian rebel contingents because (at least partially) it is seen as composed of fellow Syrians. In this light, an analysis of the feasibility of engaging in an "Awakening type" tribal mobilization-engagement strategy when confronting a group must identify the perception and image that the tribes have of the proposed targeted group.

Perhaps most importantly, the tribes in al Anbar share a number of common, overlapping identities in the province as Iraqi, as Sunni, and as Anbari. These multiple identities are often in conflict between tribes, yet they are overlapping enough that when faced with an "outside" threat, they provided enough superordinate commonality to promote cooperation. There is a history of cooperation and conflict resolution within the tribes of the region that helped formalize processes, structures, and organization in the formation of the Sahawa, the al Anbar Defense Council, and the Sons of Iraq program as detailed in the history presented in this research. All of these titles, with terms such as "Iraq," "Anbar," suggest a sense of shared identity and shared fate between and among the tribes that was reinforced, catalyzed, by a shared view of an outside threat—the foreign threat of AQI. The tribes in al Anbar had, before the Awakening, before AQI, before the US-led invasion, before the emergence of a Shi'a government in Baghdad, a sense of coalition and shared fate as Sunni tribes in al Anbar. They also had an existing framework for political negotiation between themselves. The al Anbar region is 90% Sunni, so they have a further identity on which to build beyond their already somewhat interwoven regional and tribal identity. As discussed, this identity works in opposition to the Shi'a image and perceived threat of Iranian influence. It helps to promote cooperation between the various al Anbar tribes, yet is balanced by a recognition of benefits of a working relationship with potential partners in the central government based on a history of doing so over time. These tribes also see their Sunni tribal identity as one and the same as an Iraqi identity. Nationalism, in this case, exists at the ethnic, tribal, and national level—they see themselves, as Sunni, as the rightful leaders of the state of Iraq. This perception of themselves and each other, as it relates to the fate of the country, is critically important in the motivation to fight foreign forces that may seek to usurp power and influence in their region and the state. However, as we have seen, it has powerful implications for the longer-term governance and stability of the state if they are not the group in power.

There is another matter of command and control of tribes to be considered before launching an armed tribal militia program. The tribes of the al Anbar region are much more "top down" oriented in power structure than tribes in some other regions of the world. For example, a region in which an "exportation" of the Awakening has been much discussed is Afghanistan. However, the tribes in that region do not share the type of command and control that the tribes in al Anbar have. As one noted expert explains:

> I think the word "tribe" is getting us in trouble here. Tribe doesn't mean the same thing, say, in Iraq as it does in Afghanistan, for example. In Iraq, tribes were centrally-ordered hierarchies and you could make a deal with the sheikh and the tribe would carry out the deal; that's not how a Pashtun tribe works. It's what we call a segmentary kinship system—I don't want to get into the anthropology of it but basically . . . tribe identity is what anthropologists call contingent identity (Center for a New American Security, 2009)

Tribes that do not have firm control over the actions of their members obviously present more challenges as allies in a counterinsurgency or counterterrorism strategy. In contexts of weak states, insurgency, civil war, or violent intercommunal conflict, arming and training loosely controlled and nonaligned tribal groups with conflicting or contingent identities may in fact prove counterproductive to the objective of securing a population, countering extremism, or building a state.

Relatedly, the power dynamics between tribes can often be a delicate balance. The Awakening movement had the advantage of being largely promoted from within the tribes in the region, initially. The Sahawa also enjoyed a leadership that was charismatic and at the same time sensitive to tribal politics so that it did not upset the balance between major tribes or threaten nonparticipating tribes. In regions where the tribal membership is more loosely formulated, or where tribal cooperation is necessitated by definition that some tribes will lose while others gain, or a tribal engagement policy that is not keenly sensitive to those power dynamics, it may prove exceedingly difficult to find fruitful engagement with tribes in the same way as the Sunni Awakening policy. Sattar Abu Risha, as a leader from a smaller tribe, played a unique role in balancing tribal interests and politics with overarching goals and facilitated cooperation with the central government and the United States. Any proposed replication of that policy would need at least as much leadership displaying the same kind of complexity and sensitivity to the political surroundings in order to build, maintain, and grow a similar program.

Another key feature of the Awakening movement that has been identified in Anbar was the process of protecting large population centers with tribal police forces. The Awakening was able to use local fighters to defend and police large local population centers that added to the overall security and stability to the region. Tribal regions that are less densely populated and enjoying less robust infrastructure would present larger challenges to COIN and Awakening-type strategies (Center for a New American Security, 2009).

These attributes of the Anbar province and its Sunni tribal inhabitants appear to have played a contributing factor in the initial success of the Sahawa. Any consideration of implementing a similar strategy elsewhere would benefit from a careful assessment of the proposed region shares any of these same characteristics as a basic starting point. Clearly, the dynamics in al Anbar are much more complex than the few traits listed here, and any particular comparison between al Anbar and another region would need to be much more thorough. However, identifying these key features helps frame the project.

Current events in Iraq, specifically with the advance of ISIS in Fallujah and other parts of al Anbar and Mosul Ninewa province, force consideration of the likelihood of a repeat or reemergence of the Awakening. Some important differences exist in the situation today than those existed nearly a decade ago. First, there is the concern that the Awakening movement was a response to what was largely seen as a foreign force, AQI. Our interviews of tribal leaders involved in the Awakening consistently demonstrate a perception that the tribes were confronted with foreign fighters who wanted to usurp power from them and institute a new political and social order in al Anbar, and Iraq. Reports are that ISIS is at least partly composed of former Ba'athist regime members who feel disenchanted and disenfranchised with the Maliki government. The greater this perception is that ISIS is more of an organization composed of Sunni leaders seeking to fight an unfair Shi'a government in Baghdad and not to displace or replace Sunni tribal structures in al Anbar, then, based on our findings, the less likely it is that a tribal-based resistance to ISIS is to be successful.

There exists the added complication that the al Anbar tribes have already fought a Sunni militant extremist group in AQI and, in the end, they find themselves largely marginalized and excluded from their own government. After the Awakening in which the tribes drove out the AQI presence in al Anbar, the central government rewarded them with neglect. Their political leaders were targeted by the government, and they were no longer paid for their security services once they largely removed the threat of AQI in the region, as documented above. How likely is it, then, that they are to once again come to the aid of central government, in a fresh battle against a new Sunni-dominated insurgent/extremist group? Much of that depends on if the insurgent group has changed its strategy of dealing with the tribes of the region. One of the most fatal mistakes of any actor in the story of the invasion and insurgency in Iraq is the utter and complete strategic blunder of AQI attacking the tribes of al Anbar. It may be on par with the strategic blunder of disbanding the Iraqi Army, as it contributed mightily to the Sunni tribes shifting perception of AQI from ally to barbarian, and led them to seek alliance with the United States (and the central government), fundamentally shifting the power balance in Iraq. This requires us to consider if, in fact, ISIS has adopted a new or different approach to the tribes in Iraq and al Anbar specifically.

CONCLUSIONS

This research reveals a number of perceptual changes on the part of key actors in the region of al Anbar during a period of threat, adaption, and transition. The key actors in the region, Sunni tribes and the American forces, underwent important shifts in the way they viewed each other, and these changes allowed a change in behavior. The case of the Awakening provides insights into the motivations of Sunni tribes to first initially align themselves with al Qaeda militants, or at least to see them as nonthreatening. Throughout the interviews conducted in this research, we see a clear and consistent theme of tribal leaders coping with an environment of crisis management in a sea of threats from many directions. The tribes saw the United States first as an imperialist representing an opportunity, then as a threat, and finally as an ally. They saw the AQI elements first as a nonthreatening potential ally in a changing political environment and eventually as a barbarian image, representing a dire threat and requiring the aid of an ally to successfully confront.

The interviews with coalition leaders mirror much of the same perceptual shifts. Guided by strong images of the Sunni population and tribes as rogue elements and a threat to stability, the American forces, by and large (especially at the highest levels in Washington), associated the tribes strongly with the Saddam regime. As such, US forces were initially brutally aggressive with Sunni tribes and neglected opportunities to build relationships with the tribal leadership as the tribes increasingly became engaged in violent conflict with the shared enemy of al-Qaeda. The eventual movement of the coalition to the tribes was done only when both sides were faced with repeated and clear examples of common goals and common threats. The behavior of the two actors, and the data collected through our research closely match what image theory predicts. A rogue actor is treated with a strict hand in order to elicit obedience and control. An imperial actor is approached with opportunity but also seen as an exploitative threat. A barbarian actor is seen as superior in power, lower in culture, and to confront it one needs an ally. As the two groups, American forces and Sunni tribal leaders, encountered a political reality that forced a change in their perceptions, their behavior also changed. At each stage we see behavior and statements that match the tendencies associated with various images.

Presently, the current situation al Anbar largely mirrors the situation faced by the central government, US interests, and tribal leaders at the onset of the Awakening. The ISIS forces have established footholds in the area, and made various political and tactical military gains in the region. The political dynamic between the tribes and the central government is most accurately described as one of distrust and competition. All of the features of the images and perceptions identified in the research conducted here appear to be salient once again in the current crisis. Some of the dynamics of negative images and group perceptions are likely heightened, or strengthened by the experience of a sense of abandonment expressed by the tribes after their sacrifices to confront the al Qaeda threat after the American invasion. There appears to be a sense that the tribes were "used" by the central government to fight al Qaeda, and that they were not properly rewarded for their role in defending the nation against al Qaeda. This sense of betrayal and perhaps even that of a failed enterprise in cooperation reinforce the deep negative stereotypes already strongly visible in the investigation of group relations inside al Anbar. The experience of a failed cooperation between groups with existing negative stereotypes can be severely damaging to the future relations and prospects of future positive cooperation. From a theoretical standpoint, it may be even more difficult to build a functional and effective grass-roots type fighting force in Iraq today than it was in the earliest stages of the Awakening movement.

The later post-Awakening developments in al Anbar suggest that the fundamental levels of distrust and suspicion between the major social and ethnic groups in Iraq and al Anbar remain key in resolving the overall challenge of governing Iraq as a unified nation. The research presented here provides valuable insight into understanding the core aspects of the psychological components of that political relationship and provides a way to potentially build on the limited, but effective, experiences of trust building between the major power players in Iraq. The experience of the Sahawa is frustratingly highlighted by failed opportunities to nurture positive and effective relationships between the Sunni and Shiite political groups. However, the history of the Awakening movement and the research presented here grants insight into the potential for relationship building spanning the political, ethnic, and geographic divide. The central government and the tribes are once again faced with a common enemy. Whether or not the parties can or will set aside political and religious differences to confront such a common threat remains to be seen. However, at least in this case, there is a history that both sides can turn to in helping to move forward. Whether they learn from their past cooperation in order to build a more positive relationship, or exploit lessons learned remains to be seen. The decisions made in regards to cooperation and reassessing the images held by the various groups played a key role in attaining security and stability in al Anbar and Iraq. Just as they did nearly a decade ago, the decisions made in that regard will likely have a heavy bearing on the future of stability and security in Iraq.

This history of al Anbar and the Awakening movement provides numerous lessons and insights into the significant role perceptions, social identity, and images play in policy making and security operations. The first tendencies identified in this research were the simplifications of a complex reality undertaken by perceivers. This tendency is magnified when certain images of a group are dominant. The image of a rogue involves a reduction of the complexity of the political leadership and the environment in which that leadership operates. It includes a simplification of the motivations of both leaders and followers of a rogue group, and requires a simplification of the complexities of culture and context. The consequences of these steps have been laid out in some detail in this research, but can best be summarized as a systematic failure of American leadership and military planners to properly prepare for the complex political realities on the ground in Iraq and al Anbar. It also contributed to a refusal for coalition leaders to engage Sunni tribes in the governing of Iraq and al Anbar. This refusal added to the general sense of threat the Sunni tribes experienced in a moment of profound change and instability. The consequences of the de-Ba'athification program added fuel to this fire, yet, were largely unseen or unrecognized as consequential due to an inability to recognize the cultural and political complexities of the environment. In this light, the research helps us understand the importance of recognizing and addressing the assumptions and tendencies associated with the images decision makers may hold toward a group, nation, or state. A clear lesson here is that proposed interventions or major policy changes should be accompanied by a careful consideration of the perceptual images being employed, as the assumptions of various categories have profound impact on what information and considerations will be involved in the calculus for cost, probability of success, and provide insight into existing blind spots or potential for new courses of action.

A second lesson to draw from this research is the process of image change. While these images are relatively stable, and perceivers will tend to filter information to preserve existing images, and images do change. We see a number of changes of perceptions in this book. The tribes change their perceptions of outside groups a number of times. They changed their views of the Americans three times, from imperialist with opportunity, to an imperialist presenting a threat, and finally to an ally. The tribes also shifted their perception of AQI from one of a potential ally to a barbarian actor. We contend that the tribes undertook these changes in the face of existential threats to their social identity. The evidence and reality of their situation overwhelmed the existing cognitive categorizations the tribes had developed and forced change. The evidence that their categories and perceptions were not effective and useful came in the form of increasing violence and attacks from AQI elements in their society with concurrent changes in American dealings with the tribes, first in Tal Afar and later in Ramadi. Key to this process was the openness to new information on behalf of the tribes, forced in many ways by the stark realities they faced.

In the same way, American forces underwent similar shifts. In the face of a spreading and increasingly potent insurgency and increasingly effective AQI element in al Anbar, American forces were forced into a reassessment of their strategies and tactics. This occurred at a time of important overtures made by tribal leaders seeking cooperation. The convergence of these overtures and dire security situation similarly forced a shift in perceptions. The image of the Sunni tribes as a rogue element no longer became useful and efficient as a heuristic for American forces. The evidence of a failed policy, combined with the complexities they were witnessing on the ground in the theatre of operations, led to an openness to a shift. This coincided with approaches by the al Anbar leadership. One lesson to be derived from this history is that crisis presents opportunities for shifts in perceptions. When actors are confronted with a crisis, there is an opportunity to seek or present countering information that can be used to reformulate a previously dominant perception or image. The key actors in this history responded to crisis by seeking alternative interpretations of their environment. The ability to maintain a high level of critical thinking and complexity in a crisis is vital to this process and both the American actors who played a key role in the change in tactics and the tribal leaders who approached the Americans as allies deserve credit for this cognitive flexibility in crisis. Those who resisted the shift either were eventually overwhelmed by the evidence at hand or were increasingly pushed aside by the political currents in the region. When a group is faced with dire threats (from an imperial or a barbarian, or an enemy) there is a process of seeking an ally. When a perceiver is faced with a cascading series of events that do not fit existing perceptions, there can be a process of seeking a new categorization. One story of the Awakening movement and American support is the story of how crisis points present opportunities for a change in perceptions. Successfully taking advantage of this opportunity requires an understanding of existing images.

Another lesson in this history is the significant role that policing and security forces play in effective COIN and peacekeeping operations. The failure of the American forces to emphasize a police force while focusing on rebuilding or reconstituting a military can be partially attributed to failing again to recognize complexities on the ground in al Anbar and other areas. When the US forces worked to collaborate with the people of al Anbar to build a police force, the general security in the cities began to improve, and this provided a solid foundation on which to conduct further operations against AQI. This required an interest on behalf of the Americans into the security needs and threats of the Anbari population and a concurrent building of trust between the two groups. This leads to yet another key ingredient of this experience—the process of building trust between the two groups. The interview subjects in our research and in the Marine interviews mentioned the importance of repeated meetings with US forces. While the meetings and policies were at first disjointed and inconsistent (getting a gift of a gun, then having it taken away serves as a useful example of this inconsistency), the meetings provided a common ground on which to build trust. Over time, the shared experience of repeated meetings facilitated the image shift undergone by both the US and Sunni tribal actors. An important part of this account is the mid- and ground-level leadership of the coalition and Sunni tribals maintaining contact with each other throughout the crisis, often times even without full endorsement or consent from other actors in leadership of either side.

A final lesson to be discussed here is that when important identities are threatened, members of that group will seek allies, in whatever form they see as aiding their survival or promoting the interests of their group. We can see some tribes were allying with AQI in the face of a perceived Iranian threat in Baghdad and in the face of an American invasion, especially after their initial overtures to the Americans were so roundly rejected. In al Anbar today we see again signs that ISIS is building ties and networks with some tribes in the region as their perception of threat from an Iranian-controlled Baghdad grows. This should raise the question of motivation—what is it that is happening in al Anbar that is motivating these alliances? The United States learned that if the tribal identity is threatened, the tribes will seek allies to preserve that identity and to promote their own interests. Only by providing security, and meeting the social and cultural standards of the tribes, and helping to promote a sense of involvement in the political fate of Iraq did the United States make headway into al Anbar politics and improve security. Current evidence provided above suggests that these security and political needs are not currently being met. There appears to have been a learning curve on behalf of the ISIS in terms of their dealings with the tribes, no matter how slight. The narrative identified by Gen. John Allen in our interviews that the AQI fighters represented a liberating force from an imposed political framework appears to be relevant to at least some tribes in the region today. Perhaps this lesson can be best summarized as threatened identities seek alliances. By having an awareness of those identities and how they interact or perceive threats can provide an important framework for guiding both strategic choices and tactical planning.

This research adds to the historical record of the Awakening movement by providing the perspective of the tribal leaders and Americans in the complex environment of al Anbar during the insurgency and the Awakening movement. The lessons to be learned here point to the importance of images and identity in influencing assumptions of other groups and in the behavior toward those groups. We find a consistent and congruent, mirror-like story from both the American and Sunni tribal side of perceptions and assumptions that fit behavior observed and predicted by theories of social identity and role of images in behavior. The theoretical predictions of image theory are born out in the behavior and statements by our subjects and the broader secondary data. Image shifts that we recognize in the language are matched by behavior shifts seen in the historical accounts. The accounts of our subjects match up to the theoretical explanations of the various categories of image theory. Further, more recent events in al Anbar point toward the fault lines in Iraq identified by our research. There remains a deep political divide in some aspects of the political psychology of Iraq that go as deep as tribal identity itself. Until these rifts are properly identified and addressed, the divide in Iraq is one that will dominate the political arena of the region and likely only deepen as further pressure is applied to these fractures. This is especially the case if it is exploited by fundamentalist elements operating in the region, as it appears the to be case, may be, in al Anbar presently.

NOTE

1. These include Abu Bakr al Baghdadi, Abu Ayman al-Iraqi, Abu Ahmad al Alwani, Abu Abdulrahman al Bilawi, Haji Bakr, and Abu Fatima al Jaheishi.

References

Abbas, Mushreq. (2013). Al Monitor, "Al-Qaeda sets sights on Anbar Province," http://www.al-monitor.com/pulse/originals/2013/10/anbar-valuable-for-al-qaeda.html#

Abdul-Zahra, Qassim, "Al Qaeda Forces in Iraq Take Over Fallujah and Ramadi," January 4, 2014. http://www.huffingtonpost.com/2014/01/04/al-qaeda-iraq_n_4541855.html

Abel Dadah, Ali, "Maliki Makes on De-Ba'athification", AL Monitor. (2013). http://www.al-monitor.com/pulse/originals/2013/01/maliki-quell-unrest-concessions.html?v=1362363401000?#?v=1362363401000?%29

Abu-Lughod, L. (1986). *Veiled Sentiments: Honor and Poetry in a Bedouin Society.* Berkeley: University of California Press.

al-Zarqawi, Abu Musab. (2005). "Leader of Al-Qaeda in Iraq Al-Zarqawi Declares 'Total War' on Shi'ites, States that the Sunni Women of Tel'afar Had 'Their Wombs Filled with the Sperm of the Crusaders'." Middle East Media Research Institute. September 14, 2005. Available electronically from http://hdl.handle.net/10066/4810.

Andres, M. (2010). *Adapting the Doctrinal Discourse on Campaign Planning to the Reality of Current Conflicts.* United States Army, School of Advanced Military Studies, United States Army Command and General Staff College, Fort Leavenworth, Kansas. Downloaded on December 26, 2012, from http://www.dtic.mil/dtic/tr/fulltext/u2/a522710.pdf.

Arango, Tim & Fahim Fahim, Karime. (2014). "Iraq Again Uses Sunni Tribesman in Militant War," January 19, 2014. http://www.nytimes.com/2014/01/20/world/middleeast/iraq-again-uses-sunni-tribesmen-in-militant-war.html?_r=0

Ardolino, B. (2013a). Suicide bomber kills Iraqi lawmaker who was prominent Awakening leader, and 5 others. *Long War Journal* downloaded on 5/30/2013 from http://www.longwarjournal.org/archives/2013/01/suicide_bomber_kills_74.php

Ardolino, B. (2013b). *Fallujah Awakens: Marines, Sheikhs, and the Battle against al Qaeda.* Annapolis: Naval Institute Press.

Armstrong, K. (2000). *Islam: A Short History.* New York: Random House.

Asad, T. (1970). *The Kababish Arabs: Power, Authority, and Consent in a Nomadic Tribe.* London: Hurst & Co.

Baram, A. (2005). Who are the insurgents: Sunni Arab rebels in Iraq. *Special Report*, 134: 1–20, US Institute for Peace, Washington, DC.

Beehner, L. (2006). Iraq's post-Saddam insurgency. *Backgrounder* Council on Foreign Relations http://www.cfr.org/iraq/iraqs-post-saddam-insurgency/p12007#p5 downloaded 7/12/2008.

Bin Sayeed, K. (1995). *Western Dominance and Political Islam.* Albany: State University of New York Press.

Bremer, L. P. (2006). *My year in Iraq: The struggle to build a future of hope.* New York: Simon & Schuster.

Chandrasekaran, R. (2004). Key General criticizes April attack in Fallujah. *Washington Post*, 9/13/2004.

Center for a New American Security, Senate Foreign Relations Roundtable on Afghanistan: Panelist David Kilcullen, February 5, 2009 http://www.cnas.org/media-and-events/transcripts/senate-foreign-relations-committee-roundtable-on-afghanistan-panelist-david-kilcullen-#.VS_TByk07n8.

Charrad, M. (2011). Patrimonial Power in the Modern World: State-Building in Kin-Based Societies. *The Annals of the American Academy of Political and Social Science, 636,* 49–68.

CIA Factbook. (2013).

Cole, D. (1975). *Nomads of the nomads: The Al Murrah of the empty quarter.* Chicago: Aldine Publishing Co.

Cordesman, A. (2007). Iraq's Sunni Insurgents: Looking beyond al Qa'ida. Center for Strategic and International Studies, *Working Draft*, July 26, 2007: 1–8.

Cottam, M. (1986). *Foreign policy decision-making: The influence of cognition.* Boulder, CO: Westview Press.

———. (1994). *Images and interventions: US policies toward Latin America.* Pittsburgh: University of Pittsburgh Press.

Cottam, M., Baltodano, B. & Garcia, M. (2011). Cooperation among the Sandinista factions in Nicaragua" *Latin American Policies*, *2*, 13–31.

Cottam, M. & Cottam, R. (2001). *Nationalism and politics: The political behavior of nation states.* Boulder, Lynne Rienner.

Cottam, M., Dietz-Uhler, B., Mastors, E. & Preston, T. (2010). *Introduction to political psychology,* 2nd ed. New York: Psychology Press.

Cottam, R. (1977). *Foreign policy motivation.* Pittsburgh: University of Pittsburgh Press.

Dagher, S. (2009). S.U.V.'s and rifles. Downloaded on 5/30/2012 from http://atwar.blogs.nytimes.com/2009/01/23/suvs-and-shotguns/

Dale, C. (2009). Operation Iraqi Freedom: Strategies, approaches, results, and issues for Congress. Congressional Research Service. Downloaded on June 20, 2009 from http://www.crs.gov

Dawisha, A. (1999). Identity and Political Survival in Saddam's Iraq. *Middle East Journal, 53*(4), 553–67.

Dawisha, A. (2003). *Arab nationalism in the Twentieth Century: From triumph to despair.* Princeton: Princeton University Press.

Dawisha, A. (2009). *Iraq: A political history from independence to occupation.* Princeton: Princeton University Press.

Deane, T. (2010). Providing security force assistance in an economy of force battle. *Military Review*, January–February.

Deyoung, K. (2014). Iraq's parliament speaker says Sunnis hope cooperation in Anbar crisis will yield gains. *Washington Post*, January 23, 2014. http://www.washingtonpost.com/world/national-security/iraqs-parliament-speaker-says-sunnis-hope-cooperation-in-anbar-crisis-will-yield-gains/2014/01/23/3e0c5fde-8477-11e3-8099-9181471f7aaf_story.html

Echeverria, A. (2004). *Toward an American way of war.* Strategic Studies Institute, United States Army War College.

Fields, H. (1940). The Anthropology of Iraq. *Anthropological Series, 30.*

Franks, T. (2004). *American soldier*. New York: Regan Books.

Gaertner, S., Dovidio, J. F., Anastasio, P. A., and Rust, M. C. (1993). The common in group identity model: Recategorization and the reduction of intergroup bias. In W. Stroebe, and M. Hewstone, eds., *European Review of Social Psychology, 4.* Chichester: Wiley.

Ghazi, Y & Arango, T., "Qaeda-linked militants in Iraq secure nearly full control of Fallujah" *New York Times*, January 4, 2014.

Green, D. R. (2010). The Fallujah awakening: A case study in counter-insurgency. *Small Wars Journal, 4,* 591–609.

Habib, Mustafa. (2013). "Changing alliances for 2014: a new leader for Iraq's Sunni Muslims" December 13, 2013. http://www.niqash.org/articles/?id=3344

Haddad, F. (2011). *Sectarianism in Iraq: Antagonistic visions of unity.* New York: Columbia University Press.

Hashim, A. S. (2006). *Insurgency and counter-insurgency in Iraq.* Ithaca: Cornell University Press.

Hassan, H. D. (2008). Iraq: Tribal structure, social, and political activities. *CRS Report for Congress.* Congressional Research Service: Washington, DC.

Herrmann, R. (1985a). *Perceptions and behavior in Soviet foreign policy.* Pittsburgh: University of Pittsburgh Press.

———. (1985b). Analyzing Soviet images of the United States. *Journal of Conflict Resolution, 29*, 665–697.

———. (1988). The empirical challenge of the cognitive revolution: a strategy for drawing inferences about perceptions. *International Studies Quarterly, 32,* 175–203.

———. (1991). The Soviet decision to withdraw from Afghanistan: changing strategic and regional images. In R. Jervis and J. Snyder (Eds.), *Dominoes and bandwagons* (pp. 220–49). New York: Oxford.

———, et al. (1997). Images in international relations: An experimental test of cognitive schemata. *International Studies Quarterly, 41*, 403–33.

Hersh, S. (2004). Torture at Abu Ghraib. *The New Yorker.* Downloaded on 4/1/2013 from http://www.newyorker.com.

Hersh, S. (2007). The Gneral's report. *The New Yorker*. Downloaded on 4/1/2013 from http://www.newyorker.com.

International Center for Transitional Justice (ICTJ), Briefing paper: Iraq's new accountability and justice law. January 22, 2008. http://www.iccnow.org/documents/IraqBriefingPaper_22jan08_eng.pdf

Iraq Body Count http://yubanet.com/world/Iraq-Body-Count-9-472-civilians-killed-in-2013-worst-year-since-2008-and-more-ominous.php#.UvPLZbxbtho.

Jabar, F. (2000). Shaykhs and ideologues: Detribalization and retribalization in Iraq, 1968–1998 . *Middle East Report, 215,* 28–48.

Jabar, F. (2003). Tribalization as a Tool of State Control. In F. a. Jabar, *Tribes and Power: Nationalism and Ethnicity in the Middle East.* London: Saqi Books.

Jackson, A. (2001). Images and police behavior: An analysis of police community relations. Unpublished doctoral dissertation, Washington State University, Pullman, WA.

Jensen, S. (2008). Intelligence briefing #002: Reports of infighting within the Iraqi Awakening movement. Center for Terrorism Research. Downloaded 3/26/2009 from http://www.defedemocracy.org.

Joseph, S. (2003). Gender and Family in the Arab World. In S. Sabbagh, *Arab Women: Between Defiance and Restraint.* Northampton: Olive Branch Press.

Kagan, F. (2007). Al Qaeda in Iraq: How to understand it, how to defeat it. *The Weekly Standard, 47.* Downloaded on June 2, 2010 from http://www.weeklystandard.com

Karon, T. (2004). How the prison scandal sabotages the U.S. in Iraq. *Time Magazine*, May 4. Downloaded from http://content.time.com/time/world/article/0,8599,632967,00.html. 5/11/2010.

Katzman, Kenneth, "Iraq: Politics, Governance, and Human Rights" Congressional Research Services, December 17, 2013. http://fpc.state.gov/documents/organization/219636.pdf

Kirdar, M. (2011). Al Qaeda in Iraq. *AQAM Futures Project Case Study Series,* Washington, DC: Center for Strategic & International Studies.

Kohlmann, E. (2007). State of the Sunni Insurgency in Iraq: August, 2007. Downloaded from http://www.nefafoundation.org.

Kukis, M. (2006). Turning Iraq's tribes against Al Qaeda. *Time*, December 26, downloaded on June 1, 2010 from http://www.time.com/time/world/article/0,8599,15727,00.html.

Levy, R. (1962). *The Social Structure of Islam.* London: Cambridge University Press.

Marine Corps. (2009). *Al-Anbar Awakening*. Volume I: American Perspective; Volume II: Iraqi Perspectives. Quantico, VA: Marine University Press.

McCary, J. A. (2009). The Anbar Awakening: An alliance of incentives. *Washington Quarterly*, 32, 42–59.

McKelvey, T. (2007). *Monstering: Inside America's policy of secret interrogation and torture in the terror war.* New York: Carroll & Graff Publishers.

Michaels, J. (2010). *A chance in hell.* New York: St. Martin's.

Moghaddam, F. M. (2006). *From the terrorists' point of view: What they experience and why they come to destroy.* Westport Connecticut: Praeger.

Mongomery, G. (2009). Introduction. *The Anbar awakening, volume II: Iraqi perspectives.* 1–14.

Packer, G. (2005). *The assassins' gate: America in Iraq.* New York: Farrar, Straus and Giroux.

Morris, Loveday. (2014). "To retake cities, Iraq turns to Sunni tribes." *Washington Post*, January 29. http://www.washingtonpost.com/world/middle_east/to-retake-cities-iraq-turns-to-sunni-tribes/2014/01/30/561a0a32-83b3-11e3-a273-6ffd9cf9f4ba_story.html.

Namaa, Kamal, "Fighting erupts as Iraq police break up Sunni protest camp," December 30, 2013. http://www.reuters.com/article/2013/12/30/us-iraq-violence-idUSBRE9BT0C620131230

Packer, G. (2006). The lesson of Tal Afar. *The New Yorker.* Downloaded on October 28, 2009 from http://www.newyorker.com/archive/2006/04/10/060410fa_fact2?

Parker, G. (1994). *Cross-functional teams: Working with allies, enemies, and other strangers.* San Francisco: Jossey-Bass.

Pasha, Memlik. (2014). ISIS Insurgents Have Almost Surrounded Baghdad, http://www.vice.com/en_ca/read/ISIS-Iraq-jihadists-Anbar-Fallujah-Bagdhad.

Perry, M. (2010). *Talking to terrorists: Why America must engage with its enemies.* New York: Basic Books.

Ricks, R. (2006). *Fiasco: The American military adventure in Iraq.* New York: Penguin Books.

Ricks, T. (2009). *The gamble: General David Petraeus and the American military adventure in Iraq, 2006–2008.* New York: Penguin Books.

Robinson, L. (2008). *Tell me how this ends: General David Petraeus and the search for a way out of Iraq.* New York: Public Affairs.

Roggio, B. (2007). Securing eastern Anbar Province. *The Long War Journal.* http://www.longwarjournal.org/archives.

Rumman, M. A. (2007). Iraq: The Politics of Sunni Armed Groups. *Arab Reform Bulletin, 5.*

Sakai, K. (2003). Tribalization as a Tool of State Control in Iraq: Observations of the Army, the Cabinets and the National Assembly. In F. A. Jabar and H. Dawod (eds), *Tribes and Power: Nationalism and Ethnicity in the Middle East.* London: Saqi Books.

Shane, S, & Mazzetti, R. (2008). Report blames Rumsfeld for detainee abuse. *New York Times*, December 11.

Smith, N. & MacFarland, S. (2008). Anbar Awakens: The tipping point. *Military Review,* March–April.

Spain, T. (2013) *Breaking Iraq: The ten mistakes that broke Iraq.* Palisades, NY: History Publishing Company.

Stolzoff, K. (2009). *The Iraqi Tribal System: A Reference for Social Scientists and Tribal Engagement.* Minneapolis: Two Harbors Press.

Tajfel, H. (1970). Experiments in intergroup discrimination. *Scientific American, 223*, 96–102.

———. (1978). Social categorization, social identity, and social comparison. In H. Tajfel (Ed.), *Differentiation between social groups: Studies in the social psychology of intergroup relations* (pp. 61–76). New York: Academic Press.

———. (1982). *Human groups and social categories.* Cambridge: Cambridge University Press.

Tajfel, H. & Billig, M. (1974). Familiarity and categorization in intergroup behavior. *Journal of Experimental Social Psychology, 10*, 159–170.

Todd, L., et al. (2006). *Iraq Tribal Study—al-Anbar Governorate.* Global Resources Group.

Totten, M. J. (2008). The liberation of Karmah, Part I. downloaded 5/30/2012 from http://www.michaeltotten.com/archives/2008/03/the-liberation.php

United States Marine Corps, 1MEF G-2. (2006). "State of the insurgency in al-Anbar" downloaded October 12, 2012 from http://media.washingtonpost.com/wp-srv/nation/documents/marines_iraq_document_020707.pdf.

West, B. (2005). *No true glory: A frontline account of the nettle for Fallujah*. New York: Bantam Books.

West, B. (2008). *The strongest tribe: War, politics, and the endgame in Iraq*. New York: Random House.

Whiteside, C. A. (2014). The smiling scented men: The political worldview of the Islamic State of Iraq (2003–2013). Unpublished doctoral dissertation, Washington State University, Pullman, WA.

Whiteside, C. A. (2015). ISIL's small ball warfare; An effective way to get back in the game. *War on the Rocks* downloaded 7/22/2015 from http://warontherocks.com/2015/04/isils-smallball-warfarean-effective-way-to-get-back-into-a-ballgame/?singlepage=1

Woodward, B. (2006). *State of denial: Bush at war part III*. New York: Simon & Schuster.

Index

Abu Ghraib, 39–42
al-Alwani, Mamoun, 51
al-Baghdadi, Abu Bakr, 120
Albu Mahal, 76–79
al Gaood, Jalal, 55, 63, 74
al Gaood, Talal, 56–57
Allen, John, 70, 79–80;
  on Sheikh cooperation, 96–99
ally image, 14–15
al-Maliki, Nouri, 63;
  recognition of Awakening, 97;
  sectarianism, 117–19, 123–24
al Qaeda in Iraq (AQI), 1, 59–62;
  alliance with ISIS, 115;
  entry to Iraq, 61–62;
  image change, 77, 83;
  revolt against in al Qaim, 76–79;
  split with ISIS, 120;
  violence in al Anbar, 69–74
al Qaim, 1, 19;
  awakening in, 76–79
Anbar People's Committee, 79
Awakening:
  Fallujah, 108–111;
  initial revolt against AQI, 76–79;
  philosophical versus organization, 97;
  replication of, 125–130;
  request for recognition from al Maliki, 97;
  Sattar, death of, 106;
  support from Sheikhs in exile, 81–82;
  tenets of, 93–94;
  US military objections to, 99–100, 101;
  weakening of, 121–122

Ba'athists:
  perceptions of, 31–34
barbarian image, 15, 80
Bedouin tribes, 1, 5–11
Bremer, Paul, 30–34;
  Coalition Provisional Authority, 30–33
Bush, George W., 23–34;
  axis of evil speech, 4;
  WMD and, 25–26

Casey, George W., 37, 58
Chalabi, Ahmed, 32, 49, 74
Charlton, John, 103–6;
  on Sheik Sattar, 104–6
Cheney, Dick, 27
Conway, George, 37–38, 43–45, 58
counterinsurgency strategy, 2;
  lack of, 35–39;
  McMaster, HR, 86–90;
  post-Awakening security in al Anbar, 116–117;

securing population, 99

de-Ba'athification, 30–34;
  Sunni tribal reaction to, 53–55

enemy image, 12–14

Fallujah, 19, 42–45, 56;
  Awakening spread to, 108–11;
  Blackwater killings, 43;
  Conway, George, 43–45;
  Fallujah Brigade, 34, 56

Garner, Jay, 31–32

Hadley, Steven, 26
Hamdani, Ra'ad, 48–49, 52, 57, 58, 70–71;
  on the spread of al Qaeda in Iraq, 61
Hatim, Ali, 97–98
Hussein, Saddam, 2, 6, 7, 9, 50;
  de-Ba'athification and, 30;
  rogue image and, 16, 24–27;
  tribal sheikhs, 47

images, 11–16;
  ally, 14–15;
  barbarian, 15, 80;
  change of, 85, 94–96, 130–31, 133–34;
enemy, 12–14;
imperial, 15–16, 47–49;
  rogue, 16, 24–28
imperial image, 15–16, 47–49
Iran:
  Sunni Sheikh's perception of, 74–76
Iraq:
  de-Ba'athification, 3–30;
  postwar planning for, 27–28, 35–39;
state and Sunni tribal relations, 9–11, 100
Iraqi National Insurgency, 1, 59–60
Iraqi police:
  recruitment of, 101;
  training of, 88–89, 99

ISIS, 3;
  alliance with AQ, 115;
  under Iraqi leadership, 121;
  split with AQI, 120;
  spread of, 115;
  violence and, 119–25

Karpinsky, Janice, 40–42
Khirbit, Abdulla, 53, 53

MacFarland, Sean, 79–80, 88–89, 93;
  in Ramadi, 87–89;
  spread of Awakening, 100–103;
  on tribal relations with Baghdad, 100
McMaster, H. R., 37;
  counterinsurgency planning, 84

Odierno, Ray, 37

Petraeus, David, 37
Powell, Colin, 26

Ramadi, 19, 45–46;
  Charleton on, 103–6;
  MacFarland on, 87–89
Rice, Condoleeza, 26
rogue image, 16;
  US and Sunni tribes, 65–66
Rumsfeld, Donald, 27–28

Said, Munther, 74, 82
Sanchez, Ricardo, 38, 45
Sheik Ahmed Abu Risha, 72, 123
Sheik Faisal al Gaood, 80
Sheikh Aakab al Gaood, 48, 73, 79
Sheik Hamid, Rashid, 50, 55
Sheik Hamid al Hais, 80;
  conflict with Ahmed albu Risha, 112
Sheikh Majed, 47–54, 74
Sheikh Mishan, 109–10
Sheikh Sabbah, 53, 71–72, 74, 75;
  revolt against AQI, 76–79
Sheik Sattar abu Risha, 81–82, 89, 93;
  Charleton, John, 103–6;
  death of, 106

Sheikh Shouka, 50, 53, 73;
comments on Saddam Hussein, 50
Sheikh Tariq, 48, 55, 75
social identity, 4–5;
in al Anbar, 5–11;
Sunni Sheikhs, 47–59;
threats from ISIS, 121–22;
threats to by US, 62–64
Sunni tribes, 47;
identity threat by US, 62–64;
identity threat from ISIS, 121–122;
image of al Qaeda 2003–4, 64, 80;
image of United States, 64, 90–91, 94–96;
perceptions Iraqi Shi'a, 53, 55, 74–76;
perceptions of al Qaeda, 69–70;
perceptions of Iran, 64;
perceptions of Iraqi central government, 123–124;
reaction to de-Ba'athification, 53–55

Tenant, George, 25–26

United States military:
change of images, 133–134;
change of strategy, 83–86, 99;
first Marine Expeditionary Force (1-MEF), 37, 56;
implementing new strategy, 86–90;
military force size, 28–30;
objections to Awakening, 99–100;
perception of Sunni Tribes, 65;
recruiting Sheikhs, 98–99, 100–101;
training Iraqi police, 88–89, 99

weapons of mass destruction (WMD), 25–26
Wolfowitz, Paul, 29, 31, 37

al-Zarqawi, Abu Musab, 86–87, 120, 121

About the Authors

Martha Cottam is professor of political science in the School of Politics, Philosophy, and Public Affairs, at Washington State University. She received her PhD from UCLA in 1983. Her areas of specialization include political psychology, American foreign policy, and international politics.

Joe W. Huseby is an instructor at Washington State University, in the department of Politics, Philosophy, and Public Affairs, and the Honors College. He received his PhD from Washington State University in 2013. His areas of specialization include human security, US foreign policy, and international relations

Bruno M. Baltodano is professor of political science at Florida SouthWestern State College, in Fort Myers, Florida. He received his PhD in Political Science from Washington State University in Pullman, Washington. His academic research focuses on political psychology and nationalism, primarily of indigenous groups in Nicaragua.